T0158239

KASHMIRI
CUISINE

The lofty mountains, dense and lush green forests and the colourful shikara in the serene Dal Lake makes an enchanting picture.

SARLA RAZDAN

KASHMIRI CUISINE
THROUGH THE AGES

FOREWORD
OMAR ABDULLAH

Lustre Press
Roli Books

Spinning a charkha *in the
century gone by.*

DEDICATION

The book is dedicated to Babuji who virtually adopted me as his daughter from the day I joined the Razdan family as his son's bride. He had great taste for food and enjoyed my cooking. It was he who suggested that I should write a book and was the true inspiration and my motivation behind this book. My regret is that I could not do so in his lifetime.

ACKNOWLEDGEMENTS

Many thanks to my children Nidhi, Raka and Nitin, for appreciating my culinary skills even when I thought that a dish hadn't come out very well! Their help with my laptop was immense. And, of course, my husband, M.K. Razdan without whose encouragement this book would not have been possible. Since it was first published there has been a marvellous addition to the family, Sharika. The four-year-old's taste buds are distinctly Kashmiri, believe me. Though she loves her pasta and noodles too!

And how can I forget my able lieutenants of years in the kitchen, Ram Saran and Sharvan. The only family members who aren't introduced to Kashmiri cuisine are Bruno, the Golden Retriever, and Max, the Labrador!

I am thankful to Omar for readily agreeing to write the Foreword for this edition. I suspect that his fondness for Kashmiri food has grown substantially of late, and I may have contributed to that!

CONTENTS

FOREWORD
OMAR ABDULLAH

George Bernard Shaw believed that 'there is no love sincerer than the love of food'. I can only imagine Shaw arrived at this conclusion after chancing upon a Kashmiri. A good Kashmiri has a healthy relationship with food, wherein the more you eat, the healthier that relationship. Fashionable diets are for everyone else: words like 'paleo' and 'keto', concepts like carb-cycling and Whole30, are completely alien to us. It doesn't matter if the meal is breakfast, lunch, or dinner – or, for that matter, something in between – we Kashmiris will approach it with gusto. And if there is meat to be served, then that's simply heaven on a plate.

'Kashmiri food' as a generic term is actually rather misleading as it suggests homogeneity, but that couldn't be further from the truth. Kashmiri food has more differences than similarities. There is the formal, often celebratory, food called a *wazwan*, and then there is the more regular, home-cooked food; there is the Kashmiri Muslim *wazwan* and then there is Kashmir Pandit cuisine; there are the dishes that are seasonal, and the dishes that have to be part of any and every *wazwan*.

Lastly, Kashmiri food includes those dishes specific to both a meal and a season, such as Harissa, which is specifically cooked for breakfast in the cold, winter months.

My first memories of eating a *wazwan* are of sitting with my grandparents, uncles, and aunts and being flabbergasted at the steady procession of dishes being served: the well-known Rista and Gushtaba, with the lesser known Dhaniwal Korma or coriander-flavoured meat curry, and Alubukhar Korma, or meat cooked with plums. The Alubukhar Korma remains a family favourite and you will often find my sisters and me deep-diving to dig out the cooked plums from the serving dishes. I learned a valuable lesson from my aunt at my first *wazwan*; rice is just the filler, and you eat only as much with each dish as is required to finish all the meat that is served. I'd started with the amateur mistake of gorging on the rice and filling my tummy long before the Gushtaba was served. For those of you unfamiliar with Kashmiri cuisine, the Gushtaba is the last item served by the *waza* (the chef who cooks the *wazwan*) and is popularly called 'the full-stop'.

There are a lot of myths and falsehoods associated with Kashmiri food. Yes, it's true that the love a Kashmiri has for meat is unparalleled. Kashmiris are, per capita, the highest mutton consumers in the

subcontinent, but it's not like we would refuse to eat a well-cooked vegetable. Yes, a *wazwan* is an ode, a tribute, to meat – whether it's a Muslim *wazwan* or a Pandit one, meat will be celebrated in all its glory. But there is a growing variety of vegetarian dishes that are available to choose from as well. Kashmiri Pandit food traditionally offers a greater selection of vegetable dishes, the most famous of which would have to be Dum Aloo, but let's not forget Haaq and Tchok Wangen to name but two. These days, most Muslim *wazas* will happily add a few vegetarian dishes at the request of the host.

The biggest falsehood surrounding Kashmiri food, especially dishes found in a traditional *wazwan*, is perhaps that it doesn't really lend itself to home cooking. This brings me nicely to the reason for this foreword to Sarla Razdan's *Kashmiri Cuisine: Through the Ages*. The skills required for cooking a *wazwan* are passed on by *wazas* from generation to generation. Similarly, Sarlaji honed her skills in the kitchen by first watching and then cooking with her mother. After she got married, her mother-in-law filled the void and helped her further refine her techniques and recipes.

Sarlaji is never happier than when she is cooking. Whether it's cooking for the family at home or cooking for the steady stream of friends and guests lucky enough to be invited for one of her home-cooked Kashmiri meals, she blazes a trail in the kitchen. She is a sight to see with her spices laid out in front of her and numerous pots on the cooker bubbling away. With this book, she wants to share the joy she gets from cooking Kashmiri food with all of you. Through years of practice she has refined her recipes, and what was once taught to her as 'a dash of this' and 'a pinch of that' has been simplified, so that now it's 'a teaspoon of this' and '20 grams of that'. If preparing Kashmiri food is thought to be a daunting and scary prospect, then she has taken the fear out of the cooking and left the fun intact. Now you can cook all these dishes that you've only ever read about and do so knowing that you won't go wrong.

Kashmir is so much more than just its food: it is the people, the place, the history, and the beauty that all come together to create heaven on earth. Similarly, this book is more than an attempt to pass on recipes to and preserve traditions for future generations. This book is a collection of memories, a journey through Kashmir, a collection of art and photographs. It's anything but just a cookbook. I hope you enjoy cooking and learning from it as much as I continue to enjoy eating what Sarlaji serves when I'm sitting at her table.

The wide, swift-flowing, muddy but pictureque Jhelum River sweeps through ancient Srinagar.

A flower-laden boat in the backwaters of Dal Lake.
Photograph: Steve McCurry

Author's Note

Lunch at 9 am. That is my earliest food memory from Kashmir.

When I was a little girl in Srinagar, my mother used to spend hours cooking the simplest of things like *haak* (collard greens) and *batta* (rice) for her three children. A pressure cooker was, of course, a dream.

So lunch was at nine in the morning, to arm us for the rest of the day, as we left home. Stuffed with my mother's, simple but delicious food, I then used to walk about 4 km to reach my college. In the winters, I would wake up in the morning to find three to four feet of snow all around. It used to be a lot of fun to play with the snow and we would make snowmen, putting lumps of coal for his eyes. It was freezing – but less so because our mother would wake up much before us and make sure that *kangris* (portable fire pot) were lit up and warming us by the time all of us woke up cribbing and whining.

I am a Kashmiri Pandit. We are called Saraswat Brahmins. Some are vegetarian (to the extent that they don't even have onions or tomatoes), but vast majority are voracious non-vegetarians, like most Kashmiris.

The Shivratri festival called 'Heret' in Kashmir is a big Pandit festival. Some Kashmiri Pandits – also called 'Battas' would eat meat (they were referred to as Nen (meat) Battas and also offer meat to please the gods. The vegetarian Pandits were referred to as Dal (pulses) Battas. Some Kashmiris cooked non-vegetarian food the day after the puja (*Salaam*) as on this day, their Muslim friends would come to greet them and enjoy the festivities.

My maternal home was Dal Battas and my paternal home was Nene Battas. I loved celebrating Shivratri at my maternal home (though I don't know why – as I love my meat cuisine) and I was not allowed to go to my paternal home as they were Nen Battas.

Pandit weddings were a lot of fun. Guests sat on carpets, as they still do in many Kashmiri weddings, and food was served in large *thalis* by waazas (chefs) and family members. It was the same at Muslim weddings, the only difference being the use of the large *trami* (big copper platter) to serve food (one *trami* would be shared by four people). That remains largely the tradition even now.

Atal Bihari Vajpayee

New Delhi
13th March 2008

I had the pleasure of dining with the Razdan family in New York and it was a real treat. The world is full of Indian restaurants but it is not often that one gets to taste authentic cuisine from our country. Mrs. Razdan had prepared an all-Kashmiri meal and there was a lot to choose from. I liked 'haak' saag and, among non-vegetarian dishes 'kabargah', in particular. To get such truly authentic Kashmiri food in the far off US was doubly delightful.

******

Author with the then Prime Minister Shri A.B. Vajpayee at home.

Food was served in several courses. *Kabargah* (fried breast meat) was served with pulao; likewise each dish with its flavour and delicacy was relished and appreciated separately. Liquor and wines were rarely served. *Kehwa* (Kashmiri tea) was and is still served at the weddings.

Pandits celebrate birthdays by cooking *tahar* (yellow rice), which was shared with the family — and in my childhood, the neighbourhood too — after offering it to birds or performing puja. This was one activity which I enjoyed most. Going from one home to another, I distributed yellow rice and met everyone in the process. It was real fun.

During the holy month of Ramzan, the Kashmiri Muslims were woken by a *chowkidar* (watch guard) at four in the morning, as he passed the lanes saying 'Jago!' As a child, I used to get scared, wondering why the man was shouting at 4 am. I came to know that this was the alarm for our Muslim brethren to have their meal called *sehri*. For the rest of the day, they were not supposed to eat anything, not even water, till 6 pm. A month of fasting was followed by the festival of Eid — everybody from young to old dressed in new clothes, went to mosques, and wished and greeted each other. Pandits and Muslims greeted each other, and children and ladies sang and danced the Rauf. I really miss those days.

Time passed, and I also began cooking the same Kashmiri food I had feasted on as a child. My enthusiasm for cooking really took off when I got married into a family that appreciated and enjoyed good food. My mother-in-law, Somawati, herself cooked some excellent Kashmiri dishes. My husband, M.K. Razdan, in particular, is a connoisseur. He said that I had culinary magic in my hands although he blames me whenever he puts on weight! Praise – and sometimes criticism – from my husband has always guided me towards refining my recipes, and I really thank him for that. He gave a lot of invaluable suggestions that vastly improved the book – especially the one to include low-calorie Kashmiri dishes.

I had the privilege of cooking for guests who were closely known to my husband, especially when they visited us in London and New York where we lived for several years. The little Kashmiri girl in me was mesmerized – these were names I had read only in newspapers, and now they were at our dining table, coming to compliment me in our kitchen!

I remember when Atal Bihari Vajpayee *ji* had dinner with us, I had cooked ten dishes – both vegetarian and non-vegetarian. He liked *haak* and *kabargah* and asked me, 'Did you cook all the dishes on your own?'

'Yes,' I said, beaming. He really put his hand on my head and blessed me, saying, '*Bada swadisht khanna*' (really delicious food).

When Lata Mangeshkar *ji* came to my house I was dying with excitement – my idol was coming over, in flesh and blood! I never dreamt of meeting her when I was growing up in Kashmir and listening to her songs. I have always been a great fan of hers.

And then, like a dream, there she was in the kitchen, saying, 'Can I help in any way?' Then she asked me: 'Can you make *kehwa* in a *samovar* (brass kettle)?'

I quickly answered, 'Of course!'

The grand promise came easy, but this was Manhattan – where would I get coal in

Author with the melody queen Lata Mangeshkar at her home.

Lata Mangeshkar

101, PRABHU KUNJ,
PEDDER ROAD,
MUMBAI - 400 026

FC

Kashmiri food has the reputation of being exotic, hot and essentially non-vegetarian. Some of this reputation is deserved but some is based on misconceptions. Years ago when I was invited to a Kashmiri meal by Sarla Razdan and her husband at their residence in London I asked a few questions about Kashmiri food. The Razdans had questions of their own such as: do I like spicy food? When I said yes, they appeared somewhat surprised because they thought that spicy food may not be good for my vocal cords. They offered to prepare a milder version of Kashmiri food, but I would have none of that. I said I am fond of spicy food and would love to have some 'Rogan Josh'. And did I enjoy the meal! I truly did. Later when I went to New York to perform at the Madison Square Gardens I virtually invited myself to another meal with the Razdan family which, by then, had moved there. This time no questions were asked about my preferences and I was treated to a wonderful meal again. 'Rogan Josh' and 'Kabargah' were very much on the menu. But to the delight of my sister Usha and me there were some very tasty vegetarian dishes which both of us savoured. There was the evergreen and leafy 'Haak', 'Palak and Nadroo' and amazing 'Guchhi'. Having been thus initiated into Kashmiri cuisine, I have never missed an opportunity to enjoy it at any given opportunity.

When I learnt that Sarla is doing a book on Kashmiri cuisine with emphasis on healthy food, I heartily welcomed it. We are all becoming more and more health conscious. While we must enjoy what we eat, we have to keep in mind our health. To some healthy Kashmiri food may appear to be a contradiction in terms. But that is not so as this book proves. I commend it. Read it and enjoy delightful and healthy Kashmiri cuisine.

(Lata Mangeshkar)
28·08·09

13

> " I discovered the great taste of Kashmiri food at a dinner with the Razdan family. 'Kabargah', made out of lamb's breast boiled in milk before frying, was truely mouth-watering. So was 'Yakhni', lamb cooked in yoghurt. I could not resist requesting Mrs Razdan for recipes of at least 4 of the dishes she had cooked. I tried my hand at these dishes at my home in Mumbai. I did not do a bad job but was no match to the culinary skills of Mrs Razdan! "

Author with
Sachin Tendulkar.

New York to keep the tea hot in the *samovar*, as we did back home. I managed the *kehwa* – without the coal, and she was very happy with it. Her favourite Kashmiri dishes are *rogan josh* and *kabargah* topped with a sweet dish called *shufta*.

And one fine day, I cooked all day without knowing who the guest was. It was Sachin Tendulkar! His visit – at my New Delhi home – was a huge surprise. I was not told who the guest was because I might have blabbed away to my friends, and a crowd would have collected if word spread.

After dinner, he requested me for four recipes, including *yakhni* and *kabargah*. I gave him the same recipes that I had written for this book; he tried making them at home and gave me his feedback as well. I hope my readers enjoy making them like Sachin did, hopefully with better results!

Kashimiris are hospitable by nature. We enjoy socialising and entertaining. I am no different. Frankly speaking, if one enjoys good food, then one enjoys cooking too. Cooking is my hobby, it is a great source of pleasure to cook for my family and friends.

Kashmir is unique in many ways – its natural beauty and the way Hindus and Muslims live together, notwithstanding the turbulent times the State has witnessed in recent years. We Pandits grew up in Muslim neighbourhoods. We shared the same language, the same music, and went to the same schools. Pandit and Muslim cuisines, however, are different – each special in its own way. The Muslim cuisine is overwhelmingly non-vegetarian, whereas the Pandits enjoy non-vegetarian dishes and also a wide variety of vegetarian food. A Muslim wedding in the neighbourhood provided a strong challenge to the taste buds – the Wazwaan, with over 30 varieties of meat preparation is truly a gastronomic Olympiad. Our Muslim neighbours would always invite us to savour this delightful food. For those who could not make it, food would be sent home.

When I grew up, I never stopped asking questions from my Muslim friends about how they would go about preparing such delicacies. I have included some of those recipes herein. I hope I have been able to do some justice to the reputation of Wazwaan.

I have also tried to devise innovative methods of making Kashmiri cooking simple and more adaptable without compromising on its taste.

Today, people like to eat good food, but don't have enough time to cook. I want to help our younger generation stay in touch with their finger-licking tradition of food. This book will help the younger generation (time-conscious old generation as well) to cook Kashmiri food, host parties, without investing too much time, yet keeping up with the taste.

I have also tried to introduce some dishes for the calorie-conscious readers. After all, there are a lot of myths attached to Kashmiri cuisine: that it is time consuming to make and oily to eat – tasty yet unhealthy. With this book, I have tried to iron out all these misconceptions. I have offered what I felt is an easier approach to Kashmiri cooking – a little less spice here, a little less oil there, using modern ways of cooking, and making the same centuries-old Kashmiri cooking modern and trendier.

Bon apetit!

डा. फारुक अब्दुल्ला
Dr. FAROOQ ABDULLAH

मंत्री
नवीन और नवीकरणीय ऊर्जा
भारत सरकार
MINISTER
NEW AND RENEWABLE ENERGY
GOVERNMENT OF INDIA

January 17, 2010

Kashmir is famous for its beauty, arts and craft although unfortunately it has been in the news for the wrong reason in recent years. Kashmiri food is a work of art by itself. Who does not love a 'Gushtaba' and a whole lot of other delicacies! I should know because I have been a willing 'victim' of these mouth-watering dishes. If I have any reservations about Kashmiri food it is that the best dishes are mutton based, something doctors advise not to over indulge in. Although a trained doctor myself I selectively listen to the Doctor! Such is the temptation of Kashmiri food!

I am, therefore doubly delighted that the book that Sarla Razdan has authored maintains a balance between what the doctors advise and what taste buds salivate for! Her stress on healthy Kashmiri food is welcome at a time when everyone is becoming more and more health conscious. That makes the book unique. I do intend to try out many of these recipes.

(Farooq Abdullah)

BASIC PREPARATIONS

GARAM MASALA
Makes: 500 gm / 1.1 lb

Take 250 gm / 9 oz cumin (*jeera*) seeds, 10 cloves (*laung*), 3 tbsp nutmeg (*jaiphal*) powder, 5 tbsp cinnamon (*dalchini*), 5 tbsp black cardamom (*badi elaichi*) seeds, 5 tbsp green cardamom (*choti elaichi*) seeds, 4 bay leaves (*tej patta*), 3 tbsp black cumin (*shah jeera*) seeds, 250 gm / 9 oz fenugreek seeds (*methi dana*), and 250 gm / 9 oz coriander (*dhaniya*) seeds.

Powder all these spices in a grinder and sift through a mesh cloth. Store in an airtight jar. Use as required.

VER MASALA
(Spice cake)

There are two types of *ver masala* – the one made with asafoetida is generally used in Pandit cuisine, while the other one is made with garlic and shallots and is popular in Wazwaan cooking.

Ver Masala with Asafoetida

Take ½ cup / 110 ml / 3½ fl oz mustard oil, ½ cup asafoetida (*hing*) liquid, 2 tsp salt, ½ cup red chilli powder, ½ cup / 100 gm / 3½ oz black gram (*urad dal*), ground, 2 tsp / 6 gm crushed black cumin (*shah jeera*) seeds, 2 tbsp black cardamom (*badi elaichi*) powder, 2 tbsp cinnamon (*dalchini*) powder, 2 tbsp clove (*laung*) powder, 3 tbsp cumin (*jeera*) seeds, 2 tbsp nutmeg (*jaiphal*) powder, 5 tsp / 15 gm fennel (*saunf*) powder, 50 gm / 1¾ oz ginger powder (*sonth*), 2 cups / 500 ml / 16 fl oz water, 30 gm / 1 oz coriander (*dhaniya*) powder, and 3 tsp garam masala powder.

Mix all the ingredients in a large pot. Rub in mustard oil till well incorporated. Add asafoetida liquid, gradually, rubbing and mixing really well and make a hard dough. Divide the dough equally into portions and shape each into a 3″-thick, round cake. Spread the cakes on a greased plate and sun-dry for a day, turning them once. Dry till the moisture evaporates and the cakes become stiff. Store in an airtight jar and refrigerate.

Ver Masala with Garlic and Shallots
Makes: 1 kg / 2.2 lb

Take 100 gm / 3½ oz ground garlic (*lasan*), 100 gm / 3½ oz peeled and ground shallots, 25 gm salt, 10 gm crushed black cumin (*shah jeera*) seeds, 250 gm / 9 oz ground black gram, 50 gm / 1¾ oz crushed cumin (*jeera*) seeds, 100 gm / 3½ oz ginger powder (*sonth*), 100 gm / 3½ oz fennel (*saunf*) powder, 250 gm / 9 oz coriander (*dhaniya*) seeds, 50 gm / 1¾ oz turmeric (*haldi*) powder, 150 gm / 5 oz red chilli powder, 100 gm / 3½ oz ground cloves (*laung*), ½ cup / 110 ml / 3½ fl oz mustard oil, and 1 cup / 250 ml / 8 fl oz water.

Mix all the ingredients in a deep pot along with water and knead to make a stiff dough. Divide the dough equally into small portions and shape into cakes. Dry the cakes in the sun until they have no moisture left. Store in an airtight jar. Break about 10 gm of cake and coarsely crush between the palms and add to the desired dish in the last step.

ASAFOETIDA LIQUID

Soak the asafoetida stone in warm water in a container and refrigerate. Use whenever needed.

HOME MADE YOGHURT

Take 1 lt / 32 fl oz milk & 3 tbsp / 45 gm / 1½ oz yoghurt (*dahi*).

Boil the milk, remove from heat and let it cool to room temperature. Pour in a glass jar or in a jar made of baked clay. Even pearl pet containers will do. Mix yoghurt with the milk and cover with a lid. Wrap in a shawl or old blanket for 4 hours or overnight. In summers you do not need any wrapping.

TIPS FOR CLEANING LOTUS STEMS, HAAK AND OTHER LEAFY VEGETABLES

1 Scrape lotus stems and cut into the shape desired (lotus stem is cut in different shapes for different dishes). Clean under running tap water so that all the mud comes out.
2 *Haak* is a leafy vegetable of Kashmir. Sort out leaves preferably curly ones and cut the stems out. Wash in a large pot till it is clean. You can use a pinch of potassium permaganate. Soak *haak* in potassium permaganate for 5 minutes and wash in lot of water till clean. If you cannot find *haak* you can use spinach instead.

TIPS ON HOW TO USE AND PRESERVE MUSTARD OIL

1 Heat 2 lt or 5 lt mustard oil in a large wok (*kadhai*) till smoking.
2 To check if the oil is ready to use or the smoke has gone completely put ½ peeled potato in it, if it turns brown the oil is done.
3 Let the oil cool down completely and store in a jar. Use as required. You can save lot of time by heating and storing it in advance.

SNACKS

*Tailors and embroiderers at work
under the shade of the Chinar tree
in the early twentieth century.*

Seekh Kabab

SKEWERED
MINCED LAMB

Serves: 6

INGREDIENTS

1 kg / 2.2 lb Minced meat from leg of
lamb done 5 times
3 tsp / 9 gm Red chilli powder
4 tsp Amul cheese, grated
1 tsp / 6 gm Garlic (*lasan*) paste
1 tsp / 6 gm Ginger (*adrak*) paste
3 Green chillies, cut into small pieces
1 tsp / 3 gm Black cardamom (*badi elaichi*)
powder
Salt to taste
3½ tbsp / 50 gm / 1¾ oz Butter
2 Eggs, beaten
1 tsp / 3 gm Dry mint (*pudina*)
2 tsp / 6 gm Cumin (*jeera*) powder
2 tbsp / 8 gm Green coriander (*hara
dhaniya*), chopped

METHOD

1 In a bowl, mix the mince, red chilli
powder, cheese, garlic paste, ginger paste,
green chillies, black cardamom powder,
salt, butter, eggs, mint, cumin powder,
and green coriander with your hands.

2 Take medium-sized skewers, 1″ in
diametre, and cover the middle portion
with a handful of minced meat pressing
with moist hands so that it sticks.

3 Place the skewers on charcoal fire or in a
pre-heated oven at 230°C / 450°F. Keep
checking until they are grilled all around.

4 When the kebabs are brown, slide them
slowly into a serving dish. Repeat with
the remaining mince.

5 Serve as a snack or with the main course.

Kanti

BONELESS LAMB CUBES

Serves: 6

INGREDIENTS

1 kg / 2.2 lb Lamb, boneless,
cut into 2 cm cubes, washed
3 tbsp / 45 ml / 1½ fl oz Mustard oil
500 gm / 1.1 lb Onions, peeled, cut into
4 pieces
1 cup Tomatoes, chopped
1 tsp / 3 gm Red chilli powder
1 tsp / 3 gm Ginger powder (*sonth*)
Salt to taste
1 tsp / 5 ml Lemon (*nimbu*) juice

METHOD

1 Heat the oil in a pressure cooker; add meat
cubes and semi-fry till the water dries
up. Add onions and tomatoes; stir well.
Add red chilli powder, ginger powder,
and salt; pressure cook for 5 minutes.
Remove the lid of the cooker. Add lemon
juice and simmer for 5 minutes.

2 Serve as a cocktail snack or at tea time.

Gaad Talith t, Badam

FRIED FISH WITH ALMONDS

Serves: 6

INGREDIENTS

1 kg / 2.2 lb Fish, boneless, cut into
  triangular or square pieces
Salt to taste
1 tsp / 3 gm Black pepper (*kali mirch*)
6 tbsp / 100 gm / 3½ oz Butter
½ cup / 60 gm / 2 oz All purpose flour
  (*maida*)
½ cup / 70 gm / 2¼ oz Almond (*badam*)
  flakes

METHOD

1 Wash the fish and sprinkle salt and black
   pepper. Keep aside for 1 hour.

2 Heat the butter in a frying pan; coat the
   fish with the flour and fry each side for
   3 minutes on medium heat. While frying,
   add some almond flakes.

3 Remove and garnish with slices of lemon
   and lettuce leaves.

4 Serve hot as a snack or with the main
   course.

Al Posh Mond

FRIED PUMPKIN FLOWER

Serves: 6

INGREDIENTS

250 gm / 9 oz Pumpkin flower, washed,
  drained
Salt to taste
½ tsp / 1½ gm Red chilli powder
½ cup / 60 gm / 2 oz Rice flour
2 cups / 440 ml / 15 fl oz Refined oil
  for frying

METHOD

1 Take 1 cup water in a bowl, add salt, red
   chilli powder, and rice flour. Mix well to
   make a not so thick paste.

2 Mix the pumpkin flower with the paste.

3 Heat the oil in a pan; fry the flowers until
   crispy brown. Remove and drain the
   excess oil on absorbent kitchen towels.

4 Serve as a snack with tea or cocktails or
   main course.

Wangen Pakora

FRIED AUBERGINE COATED WITH GRAM FLOUR

Serves: 6

INGREDIENTS

1 kg / 2.2 lb Aubergine (*baigan*), washed,
  cut into round thin slices
1 cup / 150 gm / 5 oz Gram flour (*besan*)
1 tsp / 3 gm Red chilli powder
Salt to taste
2 cups / 440 ml / 15 fl oz Refined oil
  for frying

METHOD

1 In a bowl, mix gram flour, red chilli
   powder, salt, and aubergine together. Add
   1 cup water and mix well to make a batter
   of normal consistency.

2 Heat the oil in a pan; fry the aubergine
   until crisp and brown. Remove and drain
   the excess oil on absorbent kitchen towels.

3 Serve hot as a snack or as an accompaniment
   with the main course.

Nadir Churma

LOTUS STEM CHIPS

Serves: 6

INGREDIENTS

1 kg / 2.2 lb Lotus stems (*kamal kakri*), cut
  into 2–3 cm-long pieces, washed, drained
3 cups / 660 ml / 21 fl oz Refined oil for
  frying
Salt to taste
¼ tsp Red chilli powder

METHOD

1 In a pot, put lotus stem and water to
   cover; boil for 10 minutes. Drain well in
   a colander and keep aside to cool.

2 Heat the oil in a deep pan; fry the lotus
   chips till crispy golden brown. Remove
   and drain on absorbent tissue paper.

3 Sprinkle salt and red chilli powder; mix
   well and serve hot as a snack or with
   main course.

Nadir Monjvor
LOTUS STEM CUTLETS

Serves: 6

INGREDIENTS

500 gm / 1.1 lb Lotus stems (*kamal kakri*),
  scraped, washed, grated
1 tsp / 3 gm Ginger powder (*sonth*)
2 tsp / 6 gm Red chilli powder
Salt to taste
2 tbsp / 20 gm Rice flour / Corn flour
1 cup / 220 ml / 7 fl oz Refined oil
  for frying

METHOD

1 Squeeze the water out of the grated lotus stems.

2 In a bowl, mix the grated lotus stem, ginger powder, red chilli powder, salt, and rice flour together.

3 Divide the mixture into equal portions and shape into small balls and flatten slightly.

4 Heat the oil in a frying pan; fry these cutlets till crispy brown, turning once or twice. Repeat with the remaining balls.

5 Serve hot as a snack or with the main course.

Top: Gujjar women.
Below: Kashmiri papier maché merchant from 1890s.

23

*A picturesque autumn in Srinagar when the green
leaves turn to gold and then to russet and red.
Photograph: Mukhtar Ahmad*

Silver and coppersmiths chasing, gliding and polishing decorative articles like tea sets, tumblers, boxes, and more in the early days.

Lamb

28 MACH SHYAMI
Minced lamb cutlets in yoghurt

29 MACHGAND
Minced lamb fingers

30 MACH T, CHER
Lamb fingers with apricot

31 OLUV BUKHARA
BARITH MACH
Apricot stuffed meat balls

32 METHI T GOLEMACH
Lamb balls in fenugreek sauce

32 MACH T, MACARONI
Minced lamb in macaroni

33 MACH BARITH
KAREL
*Bitter gourd stuffed with
minced lamb*

33 MACH T, PHOOL
Lamb fingers with cauliflower

35 MACH T, OLUV
*Lamb fingers cooked
with potatoes*

36 METHI T, SYUN
Fenugreek cooked with lamb

36 MUNJ T, SYUN
Knol khol cooked with lamb

37 YAKHNI
Lamb cooked in yoghurt

38 GUSHTABA
Lamb balls in yoghurt gravy

39 RISTA
Lamb balls in red gravy

42 PALAK T, RISTA
*Lamb balls cooked with
spinach*

43 KABARGAH
*Lamb chunks decorated
with silver leaf*

43 AAB GOSHT
Lamb in milk gravy

46 DHANIWAL KORMA
*Lamb in coriander
flavoured gravy*

46 ALUBUKHAR
KORMA
Lamb cooked with plums

47 PALAK T, SYUN
Spinach cooked with lamb

47 GOLE AL SYUN
Pumpkin cooked with lamb

48 KALIYA
Lamb in yellow gravy

48 ROGAN JOSH
Lamb in red gravy

49 GOGJI T, SYUN
Lamb with turnips

49 VOST HAAK T, SYUN
Green / red leaves with lamb

52 OLUV T, SYUN
*Potatoes and lamb in
thick gravy*

52 CHAMP
Lamb chops

53 BUKVETCH CHAGIL
T, CHARVAN
Spicy kidneys, testes and liver

53 TCHOKH CHARVAN
Tangy liver

55 PACHH ROGAN JOSH
Trotter in red gravy

55 PACHH RAS
Trotter soup

Mach Shyami

MINCED LAMB CUTLETS IN YOGHURT

Serves: 6–10

INGREDIENTS

1 kg / 2.2 lb Minced lamb
3 tsp / 9 gm Fennel (*saunf*) powder
2 tsp / 6 gm Ginger powder (*sonth*)
½ cup / 110 ml / 3½ fl oz Mustard /
  Refined oil
Salt to taste
½ tsp Asafoetida (*hing*)
3 Cloves (*laung*)
2 Bay leaves (*tej patta*)
2 pieces Cinnamon (*dalchini*) sticks
2 tsp / 6 gm Cumin (*jeera*) powder
3 cups / 675 gm / 24 oz Yoghurt (*dahi*),
  whisked
3 Black cardamoms (*badi elaichi*)
4 Green cardamoms (*choti elaichi*)
2 tsp / 5 gm Black cumin (*shah jeera*) seeds

METHOD

1 In a large bowl, mix the minced meat with 1 tsp fennel power, ½ tsp ginger powder, and ½ tsp salt. Divide the mixture into two to three portions and shape into 4″-long rolls.

2 Boil 8 cups water separately in a large vessel, put the rolls in the water carefully so that they don't break. Boil until the rolls are hard; remove the vessel from the heat and keep aside to cool.

3 Take the rolls out of the vessel and preserve the stock. Cut these rolls into 1½″ round cutlets.

4 Heat the oil in a deep vessel; add salt, asafoetida, cloves, bay leaves, and cinnamon sticks. Add the preserved stock and the remaining fennel powder, ginger powder and cumin powder; bring the mixture to the boil.

5 Add the whisked yoghurt to the gravy and let it boil until the gravy thickens.

6 Add the minced meat cutlets to the mixture and bring to the boil.

7 Grind black cardamoms and green cardamoms together, along with the skin. Add to the gravy along with black cumin seeds; mix well.

8 Serve hot with steamed rice, chapatti or *nan*.

Note: This dish is served on very special occasions, like weddings and festivals.

Machgand
MINCED LAMB FINGERS

Serves: 6-10

INGREDIENTS

1 kg / 2.2 lb Minced meat from leg of lamb
3 tsp / 9 gm Red chilli powder
2 tsp / 6 gm Ginger powder (*sonth*)
3 tsp / 9 gm Fennel (*saunf*) powder
Salt to taste
4 Black cardamoms (*badi elaichi*)
3 tsp / 9 gm White cumin seed powder
1 cup / 220 ml / 7 fl oz Mustard oil
¼ tsp Asafoetida (*hing*) liquid (see p. 17)
2 Bay leaves (*tej patta*)
2 Cloves (*laung*)
3 Green cardamoms (*choti elaichi*)

A flower seller on the Dal Lake at winter time.

METHOD

1 Mix the minced meat with 1 tsp red chilli powder, ½ tsp ginger powder, 1 tsp fennel powder, 1 tsp salt, 3 ground black cardamom, 1 tsp cumin powder, and 3 tbsp mustard oil in a large bowl. Marinate for 10 minutes.

2 Divide the mixture equally into 25 portions and shape into 1½″-long fingers.

3 Heat the remaining mustard oil in a deep vessel. Add salt, asafoetida liquid, bay leaves, cloves, 1 cup water, and remaining red chilli powder.

4 Keep stirring on high heat until the water is absorbed and the mixture turns red. Pour 6 cups water and add remaining spice powders and salt to taste; bring to the boil.

5 Add minced meat fingers, one by one, into the gravy. Let it boil on high heat until it leaves oil.

6 Coarsely grind green cardamom and 1 black cardamom together and add to the vessel; mix. Serve hot.

Note: Chilli and salt can be altered to taste without spoiling the delicate flavour of this dish. If you are unable to shape the mince into fingers, round balls can be made instead.

Mach t, Cher

LAMB FINGERS WITH APRICOT

Serves: 6-10

INGREDIENTS

1 kg / 2.2 lb Minced lamb
500 gm / 1.1 lb Yellow dried apricot
  (*khubani*), washed in lukewarm water
1 cup / 220 ml / 7 fl oz Mustard /
  Refined oil
2 tsp / 6 gm Ginger powder (*sonth*)
3 tsp / 9 gm Red chilli powder
3 tsp / 9 gm Fennel (*saunf*) powder
Salt to taste
2 tsp / 6 gm White cumin seed powder
3 Black cardamoms (*badi elaichi*)
½ tsp Asafoetida (*hing*) liquid (see p. 17)
2 Cinnamon (*dalchini*) sticks
1 Bay leaf (*tej patta*)
2 Cloves (*laung*)

METHOD

1 Mix the minced meat with 3 tbsp oil, ½ tsp ginger powder, 1 tsp red chilli powder, 1 tsp fennel powder, 1 tsp salt, and 1 tsp cumin powder in a large bowl.

2 Coarsely grind 2 black cardamoms and add to the mixture. Mix well and keep aside to marinate for 10 minutes.

3 Divide the mixture equally into portions and shape into 1½″-long fingers.

4 Heat the remaining oil in a large vessel; add salt, asafoetida liquid, cinnamon sticks, bay leaf, remaining red chilli powder, and ½ cup water. Stir until a red colour appears.

5 Add 6 cups water and the remaining spice powders.

6 When the gravy starts boiling, add the meat fingers slowly so that they don't break. Boil on high heat until the gravy thickens.

7 Add apricots and boil for 2 more minutes. Reduce heat and simmer for 5 minutes and serve.

Note: This dish looks beautiful when laid on the table as the apricots remain yellow and the minced meat red making it very colourful.

Oluv Bukhara Barith Mach

MINCED MEAT BALLS STUFFED WITH APRICOT

Serves: 6-10

INGREDIENTS

1 kg / 2.2 lb Minced lamb

500 gm / 1.1 lb Dried apricots (*khubani*), round ones, soaked for 30 minutes in warm water, deseeded

1 cup / 220 ml / 7 fl oz Mustard / Refined oil

2 tsp / 6 gm Ginger powder (*sonth*)

3 tsp / 9 gm Red chilli powder

3 tsp / 9 gm Fennel (*saunf*) powder

Salt to taste

2 tsp / 6 gm White cumin seed powder

3 tsp / 9 gm Black cardamom (*badi elaichi*) powder

½ tsp Asafoetida (*hing*) liquid (see p. 17)

2 Bay leaves (*tej patta*)

2 Cinnamon (*dalchini*) sticks

METHOD

1 Mix the minced meat with 3 tbsp oil, ½ tsp ginger powder, 1 tsp red chilli powder, 1 tsp fennel powder, 1 tsp salt, 1 tsp cumin powder, and 1½ tsp black cardamom powder. Marinate for 20 minutes

2 Divide the mixture equally into portions and shape into round balls, stuffing an apricot into each ball.

3 Heat the remaining oil in a vessel; add salt, asafoetida liquid, a little water, and 2 tsp red chill powder; bring to the boil until the mixture turns red.

4 Add 6 cups water and the remaining spice powders. When the gravy is boiling, add the meat balls gradually so that they don't break. Boil until the gravy thickens. Add the remaining cardamom powder and simmer for 5 minutes. Serve hot.

A shikara ride at sunset on the Dal Lake is an unforgettable experience.
Photograph: Mukhtar Ahmad

Methi t, Golemach

MINCED MEAT BALLS WITH FENUGREEK

Serves: 6-8

INGREDIENTS

1 kg / 2.2 lb Minced lamb
6 tsp Dried fenugreek (*kasoori methi*)
Salt to taste
1 tsp / 3 gm Ginger powder (*sonth*)
3 tsp / 9 gm Fennel (*saunf*) powder
3 tsp / 9 gm Red chilli powder
2 Black cardamoms (*badi elaichi*)
3 Green cardamoms (*choti elaichi*)
2 tsp / 6 gm White cumin seed powder
1 cup / 220 ml / 7 fl oz Mustard / Refined oil
1 Bay leaf (*tej patta*)
½ tsp Asafoetida (*hing*)
3 Cloves (*laung*)
2 Cinnamon (*dalchini*) sticks

METHOD

1 Mix the minced meat with 1 tsp salt, ½ tsp ginger powder, 1 tsp fennel powder, 1 tsp red chilli powder, 1 crushed black cardamom, 2 crushed green cardamoms, 1 tsp cumin powder, and 2 tbsp oil in a large bowl. Mix well and marinate for 10 minutes.

2 Divide the mixture equally into portions and shape into 1″-thick balls.

3 Heat the remaining oil in a pot; add bay leaf, asafoetida, cloves, cinnamon sticks, salt to taste, 1 cup water, and 2 tsp red chilli powder. Keep stirring until the mixture turns red.

4 Add 6 cups water and remaining spice powders except the fenugreek powder. Bring the mixture to the boil. Add the meat balls gradually so that they don't break.

5 Boil until the gravy thickens. Add the fenugreek powder and simmer for 5 minutes. Serve hot.

Mach t, Macaroni

MINCED LAMB IN MACARONI

Serves: 6-10

INGREDIENTS

1 kg / 2.2 lb Minced lamb
1 cup / 100 gm / 3½ oz Macaroni, cut, soaked in warm water for 5 minutes, drained in a colander
½ cup / 110 ml / 3½ fl oz Refined oil
1 Clove (*laung*)
1 Cinnamon (*dalchini*) stick
2 cups Tomatoes, fresh, chopped OR
400 gm / 14 oz Tomato purée
Salt to taste
3 tsp / 9 gm Red chilli powder
1 tsp / 3 gm Ginger powder (*sonth*)
3 tsp / 9 gm Cumin (*jeera*) powder
2 tsp / 6 gm Black cardamom (*badi elaichi*) powder

METHOD

1 Heat the oil in a deep vessel; add clove, cinnamon stick, and mince. Fry until the water dries up. Add chopped tomatoes or tomato purée. Keep stirring. Add salt, red chilli powder, ginger powder, cumin powder, and black cardamom powder; mix well. Add 6 cups water and bring the mixture to the boil.

2 Add macaroni and mix well. Bring to boil again for 10 minutes. Simmer for 5 minutes and serve with *nan*, chapatti or rice.

Note: Make sure you buy long-cut macaroni. To prevent the macaroni from getting too soggy keep checking from time to time.

Mach Barith Karel

BITTER GOURD STUFFED WITH MINCED LAMB

Serves: 6

INGREDIENTS

500 gm / 1.1 lb Minced lamb
12 Bitter gourd (*karela*), scraped, slit
  lengthwise keeping shape intact, deseeded
½ cup / 110 ml / 3½ fl oz Mustard /
  Refined oil for frying
¼ tsp Asafoetida (*hing*)
Salt to taste
2 tsp / 6 gm Red chilli powder
2 tsp / 6 gm Ginger powder (*sonth*)
2 tsp / 6 gm Cumin (*jeera*) powder

METHOD

1 Sprinkle salt on the bitter gourd and keep
  aside for an hour. Wash it under running
  water and squeeze well.

2 Heat the oil in a pan; shallow-fry the
  bitter gourd until golden brown. Remove
  and cool.

3 Heat 2 tbsp oil in a pan; add asafoetida,
  salt to taste, and minced meat. Fry until
  the mince turns light brown. Add all the
  powdered spices and ½ cup water; mix well
  with a ladle and cook till the water dries
  up. Remove.

4 Stuff the fried bitter gourd with the mince
  and serve with chapatti, *nan* or rice.

Mach t, Phool

MINCED LAMB FINGERS WITH CAULIFLOWER

Serves: 6-8

INGREDIENTS

1 kg 2.2 lb Minced lamb
500 gm / 1.1 lb Cauliflower (*phool gobi*), cut
  into medium-sized florets, washed, drained
3 tsp / 9 gm Red chilli powder
3 tsp / 9 gm Fennel (*saunf*) powder
2 tsp / 6 gm Ginger powder (*sonth*)
Salt to taste
2 tsp / 6 gm Cumin (*jeera*) powder
1 cup / 220 ml / 7 fl oz Mustard /
  Refined oil
¼ tsp Asafoetida (*hing*)
2 Cloves (*laung*)

METHOD

1 Mix the mince with 1 tsp red chilli powder,
  1 tsp fennel powder, 1 tsp ginger powder,
  1 tsp salt, 1 tsp cumin powder, 3 tbsp oil in
  a large bowl and keep aside for 30 minutes.

2 Divide the mixture and shape into 1½˝-thick
  fingers.

3 Heat the oil in a large vessel; add salt,
  asafoetida, cloves, 2 cups water, and
  remaining red chilli powder. Keep stirring
  till the mixture turns red. Add 6 cups water
  and remaining spice powders. Bring to
  the boil.

4 Add the minced fingers, one by one so that
  they don't break. Cook for 15 minutes over
  high heat.

5 Fry the cauliflower light brown in a separate
  pan and add to the mixture. Cook for
  5 minutes and serve
  with rice, *nan* or
  chapatti.

Methi t, Syun

FENUGREEK COOKED WITH LAMB

Serves: 6

INGREDIENTS

1 kg / 2.2 lb
  Lamb, boneless,
  cut into cubes, washed
1 kg / 2.2 lb Fenugreek (*methi*), cleaned,
  washed, drained
1 cup / 220 ml / 7 fl oz Mustard oil
½ tsp Asafoetida (*hing*) liquid (see p. 17)
2 Cloves (*laung*)
2 Cinnamon (*dalchini*) sticks
2 Bay leaves (*tej patta*)
3 tsp / 9 gm Red chilli powder
1 tsp / 3 gm Turmeric (*haldi*) powder
Salt to taste
2 tsp / 6 gm Ginger powder (*sonth*)
3 tsp / 9 gm Fennel (*saunf*) powder
2 tsp / 6 gm Black cardamom (*badi elaichi*)
  powder
2 tsp / 6 gm Cumin (*jeera*) powder

METHOD

1 Boil the fenugreek in a vessel until tender.

2 Heat the oil in a pressure cooker; add
   asafoetida liquid, cloves, cinnamon stick,
   bay leaves, and meat. Fry the meat until
   golden brown.

3 Add red chilli powder, turmeric powder,
   2 cups water, and salt to taste; stir with a
   ladle over high heat. Add fenugreek and
   remaining spice powders; mix well. Pressure
   cook for 10 minutes or after 2 whistles.

4 Remove the lid and check if the meat is
   tender, cook until the gravy thickens.

5 Serve hot with rice, chapatti or *nan*.

Munj t, Syun

KNOL KHOL COOKED WITH LAMB

Serves: 6

INGREDIENTS

1 kg / 2.2 lb Lamb cut from breast and
  shoulder, washed
500 gm / 1.1 lb Knol khol (*kholrabi*), peeled,
  cut into 4 pieces, leaves washed, drained
½ cup / 110 ml / 3½ fl oz Mustard /
  Refined oil
Salt to taste
½ tsp Asafoetida (*hing*) liquid (see p. 17)
3 tsp / 9 gm Fennel (*saunf*) powder
1½ tsp / 4½ gm Ginger powder (*sonth*)
1½ tsp / 4½ gm Turmeric (*haldi*) powder

METHOD

1 Heat the oil in a pressure cooker; add salt,
   asafoetida, and lamb. Fry for 10 minutes.
   Add knol khol along with the leaves; cook
   for another few seconds.

2 Pour 6 cups water and add the spice powders.
   Pressure cook for 10 minutes and remove
   the lid.

3 Serve with steamed rice.

Yakhni

LAMB COOKED IN YOGHURT

Serves: 6

INGREDIENTS

1 kg / 2.2 lb Lamb cut from breast and
  shoulder with bones, cleaned
½ cup / 110 ml / 3½ fl oz Mustard /
  Refined oil
1 Cinnamon (*dalchini*) stick
3 Black cardamoms (*badi elaichi*)
4 Green cardamoms (*choti elaichi*)
2 Bay leaves (*tej patta*)
2 Cloves (*laung*)
3 tsp / 9 gm Fennel (*saunf*) powder
2 tsp / 6 gm Ginger powder (*sonth*)
Salt to taste
3 cups / 675 gm / 24 oz Yoghurt (*dahi*)
1 tsp / 5 gm Corn flour / Rice flour
1 tsp / 2½ gm Black cumin (*shah jeera*) seeds

METHODS

1 Heat the oil in a pressure cooker; add
   cinnamon stick, 1 black cardamom, 2 green
   cardamoms, bay leaves, cloves, and lamb.
   Fry for 10 minutes.

2 Pour 6 cups water and add fennel powder,
   ginger powder, and salt to taste. Pressure
   cook for 10 minutes or till 2 whistles.
   Remove the lid when the pressure drops
   and check if the meat is tender. Pour the
   stock out from the pressure cooker into a
   separate vessel and keep the meat pieces
   inside.

3 Whisk the yoghurt in a bowl. Add to the
   stock, stirring with a ladle, and cook until
   it starts boiling. Add the cooked meat and
   cook until the gravy thickens.

4 Whisk 1 tsp corn flour or rice flour in 4 tsp
   water. Add to the meat mixture (this helps
   in thickening the gravy).

5 Coarsely grind 2 black and 2 green
   cardamoms, and add to the gravy. Sprinkle
   black cumin seeds (this gives a wonderful
   flavour). Serve hot with steamed rice.

Note: This is Sachin Tendulkar's favourite dish.

Gushtaba

LAMB BALLS IN YOGHURT GRAVY

Serves: 6-8

INGREDIENTS

1 kg / 2.2 lb Lamb, boneless from leg
250 gm / 9 oz Meat fat / White butter
3 Black cardamoms (*badi elaichi*)
1 tsp / 3 gm Ginger powder (*sonth*)
Salt to taste
10 bones Lamb stock
12 cups / 3 lt Water
½ cup / 100 gm / 3½ oz Ghee
1 tsp / 6 gm Garlic (*lasan*) paste
2 tsp / 6 gm Fried onion paste
2 Cloves (*laung*)
1 Cinnamon (*dalchini*) stick
5 Green cardamoms (*choti elaichi*)
2 Bay leaves (*tej patta*)
3 tsp / 9 gm Fennel (*saunf*) powder
2 cups / 480 ml / 16 fl oz Milk
2 cups / 450 gm / 1 lb Yoghurt (*dahi*)
2 tsp / 6 gm Dried mint (*pudina*)

METHOD

1 Pound the boneless meat on a smooth stone with a wooden mallet. Add meat fat / white butter, 2 ground black cardamoms, ginger powder, and salt. Keep pounding until you get a smooth pulp.

2 Divide the mixture into equal portions and shape into round balls. Keep aside.

3 Boil the bones in 12 cups water for 30 minutes and strain, keep the stock aside.

4 Heat the ghee in a large vessel; add salt, garlic paste, fried onion paste, cloves, cinnamon stick, green cardamom, 1 black cardamom, and bay leaves. Add the stock and keep stirring. Add fennel powder, milk, and whisked yoghurt; mix well. Add the lamb balls called *gushtabas*, one by one, and boil for 30 minutes or until the balls are tender and the gravy is thick. Simmer for about 15 minutes.

5 Sprinkle dried mint and serve hot with steamed rice.

Note: For the diet conscious and those with no time to cook in the traditional way, here are a few tips to make this dish easy.
- *Use a grinder instead of stone and wooden mallet.*
- *Add egg whites instead of meat fat. Or use unsalted butter.*
- *Red meat can be replaced with boneless chicken.*

Rista

LAMB BALLS IN RED GRAVY

Serves: 6

INGREDIENTS

1 kg / 2.2 lb Lamb, boneless, fresh cut
   from leg
250 gm / 9 oz Meat fat / White butter
10 Bones to make stock
½ cup / 100 gm / 3½ oz Ghee
Salt to taste
2 tsp / 6 gm Red chilli powder
3 Cloves (*laung*)
10 Green cardamoms (*choti elaichi*)
1 tsp / 6 gm Garlic (*lasan*) paste
2 tsp / 6 gm Fried onion paste
2 tsp / 6 gm Turmeric (*haldi*) powder
¼ tsp Saffron (*kesar*)
½ cup Dry cockscomb (*mawal*) extract
   (see note below)

METHOD

1 Pound the boneless meat on a smooth
   stone with a wooden mallet as in *gushtaba*.
   Add meat fat / white butter while
   pounding. Make sure the pulp is mixed
   enough to shape into equal-sized round
   balls called *ristas*. Keep aside.

2 Boil the bones separately for 30 minutes
   to make stock.

3 Heat the ghee in a large vessel; add, salt,
   stock, red chilli powder, cloves, green
   cardamoms, garlic paste, onion paste, and
   turmeric powder. Keep stirring until the
   mixture turns red. Add about 15 cups
   water and bring to the boil.

4 While the gravy is boiling, add the meat
   balls slowly. Boil for an hour. Add dry
   cockscomb or saffron extract. Simmer for
   5-10 minutes.

5 Serve hot with steamed rice.

*Note: *Mawal (cockscomb) is a dried flower available
only in Kashmir. This is generally used for colouring.
Mawal extract is made by soaking the flower in
1 cup water for about an hour. Since this may not be
easily available, saffron extract is a good substitute.
½ tsp saffron soaked in 1 cup water can be used for
this dish.*

*Popular Avenue – en route to Gulmarg in
the 1930s.*

A fisherman casting a net in the Dal lake – home to plenty of fishes. Fishing is the second largest industry in Srinagar and hence the main source of occupation for majority of inhabitants around the lake.

Palak t, Rista

LAMB BALLS COOKED WITH SPINACH

Serves: 6

INGREDIENTS

1 kg / 2.2 lb Minced lamb, mince done as in *Rista*

1 kg / 2.2 lb Spinach (*palak*), washed, boiled, drained

½ cup / 110 ml / 3½ oz Refined oil

3 tsp / 9 gm Red chilli powder

Salt to taste

2 tsp / 6 gm Ginger powder (*sonth*)

2 tsp / 6 gm Turmeric (*haldi*) powder

3 tsp / 9 gm Garlic (*lasan*) paste

2 Cinnamon (*dalchini*) sticks

4 Green cardamoms (*choti elaichi*), crushed

2 tsp / 6 gm Black cardamom (*badi elaichi*) powder

¼ cup Dry cockscomb (*mawal*) extract (see p. 39)

1 tsp / 2½ gm Black cumin seeds (*shah jeera*)

METHOD

1 Make round balls of the minced meat weighing 10 gm each.

2 Heat the oil in a deep vessel; add red chilli powder, salt, 8 cups water, ginger powder, turmeric powder, garlic paste, and cinnamon sticks. Bring to the boil. Add lamb balls and cook for 30 minutes on high heat.

3 Squeeze water out of boiled spinach and crush with hands. Add to above mixture; mix well. Add crushed green cardamoms, black cardamom powder and cockscomb extract; cook until the gravy thickens.

4 Serve hot with steamed rice.

Kashmiri Hindu pandits in the 1890s.

42

Kabargah

FRIED BREASTS OF LAMB

Serves: 6

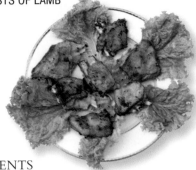

INGREDIENTS

1 kg / 2.2 lb Breast of Lamb, cut into square
/ rectangle pieces, washed
3 cups / 750 ml / 24 fl oz Water
3 cups / 720 ml / 23 fl oz Milk
2 Bay leaves (*tej patta*)
2 Cloves (*laung*)
2 Cinnamon (*dalchini*) sticks
2 Black cardamoms (*badi elaichi*)
5 Green cardamoms (*choti elaichi*)
1 tsp / 3 gm Cumin (*jeera*) powder
½ tsp / 1½ gm Ginger powder (*sonth*)
½ tsp / 1½ gm Fennel (*saunf*) powder
Salt to taste
½ tsp Saffron (*kesar*)
1 cup / 220 ml / 7 fl oz Ghee / Refined oil
2 portions Silver leaves (*varq*) (optional)

METHOD

1 Cook the meat in a deep vessel. Add water,
milk, and all the ingredients except oil.
Cover and cook until the meat is tender.

2 Remove the lid and check if the meat is
tender. Boil until the gravy is absorbed and
the meat is tender.

3 Remove the meat pieces, one by one, with
a tong so that they don't break. Separate
them in a large plate.

4 Heat the oil in pan; fry the meat, 2-3 pieces
at a time, until light brown.

5 Serve hot as a snack or with main course.

Aab Gosht

LAMB IN MILK GRAVY

Serves: 6

INGREDIENTS

1 kg / 2.2 lb Lamb, cut from shoulder, washed
½ cup / 110 ml / 3½ oz Refined oil
3 Cloves (*laung*)
5 Green cardamoms (*choti elaichi*), crushed
3 tsp / 9 gm Fennel (*saunf*) powder
2 tsp / 12 gm Fried onion paste
2 tsp / 12 gm Garlic (*lasan*) paste
3 cups / 720 ml / 23 fl oz Full-cream milk,
boiled
Salt to taste

METHOD

1 Add 8 cups water in a deep vessel and boil
the lamb for 5 minutes. Drain the stock in
another pot.

2 Wash lamb in cold water and add to the
stock.

3 Heat the oil in a pressure cooker; add
cloves, lamb with stock, green cardamoms,
fennel powder, fried onion paste, and garlic
paste. Pressure cook for 5 minutes. Open
the lid when the pressure drops to check if
the meat is tender.

4 Add milk and mix well. Boil until the
gravy thickens.

Embroiderers at work. Designs such as the paisley motifs, lotuses, chinar leaves, birds and flowers are stitched by hand in fine silk threads on woollen garments and shawls.

Dhaniwal Korma

LAMB IN CORIANDER FLAVOURED GRAVY

Serves: 6

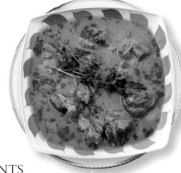

INGREDIENTS

1 kg / 2.2 lb Lamb, cut from leg, washed
1 cup / 220 ml / 7 fl oz Refined oil
3 Cloves (*laung*)
3 tbsp Fried onion paste
1 tsp / 6 gm Garlic (*lasan*) paste
Salt to taste
6 Green cardamoms (*choti elaichi*), crushed
1 tsp / 3 gm Turmeric (*haldi*) powder
2 tsp / 6 gm Coriander (*dhaniya*) powder
½ tsp Saffron (*kesar*) extract
2 cups / 450 gm / 1 lb Yoghurt (*dahi*), whisked
½ cup / 30 gm / 1 oz Green coriander (*hara dhaniya*), chopped

METHOD

1 Boil the lamb in a deep vessel for 5 minutes; drain the stock and keep aside.

2 Wash the lamb in cold water and keep aside.

3 Heat the oil in a pressure cooker; add the cloves, onion paste, garlic paste, salt, green cardamoms, and the lamb; mix well. Add the stock, turmeric powder, coriander powder, and saffron extract; pressure cook for 5 minutes.

4 When the pressure drops, check if the lamb is tender. Add yoghurt and mix well with a ladle. Cook over high flame until the gravy thickens.

5 Serve hot garnished with green coriander.

Alubukhar Korma

LAMB COOKED WITH PLUMS

Serves: 6

INGREDIENTS

1 kg / 2.2 lb Lamb, boneless, cut from leg
1 cup Dried plums (*alubukhara*), washed and soaked
1 cup / 220 ml / 7 oz Refined oil
3 Cloves (*laung*)
Salt to taste
2 Cinnamon (*dalchini*) sticks
6 Green cardamoms (*choti elaichi*), crushed
3 tsp / 9 gm Red chilli powder
1 tsp / 3 gm Turmeric (*haldi*) powder
½ cup / 100 ml / 3½ fl oz Tamarind (*imli*) liquid
1 tsp / 6 gm Garlic paste

METHOD

1 Heat the oil in a pressure cooker; add the lamb, cloves, salt, cinnamon sticks, and green cardamoms. Fry until golden brown.

2 Add red chilli powder, turmeric powder, and 6 cups water; pressure cook for 10 minutes.

3 Open the lid when the pressure drops and add the dried plums and tamarind liquid; cook until the gravy thickens. Mix well and cook over low heat until the plum is soft.

4 Serve hot with boiled rice.

Palak t, Syun

SPINACH COOKED WITH LAMB

Serves: 6

INGREDIENTS

1 kg / 2.2 lb Lamb, boneless, preferably
2 kg / 4.4 lb Spinach (*palak*), stems removed,
  cleaned, washed thoroughly
1 cup / 220 ml / 7 fl oz Mustard oil
Salt to taste
½ tsp Asafoetida (*hing*)
500 gm / 1.1 lb Tomatoes, chopped
4 tsp / 12 gm Red chilli powder
2 tsp / 6 gm Ginger powder (*sonth*)
2 tsp / 6 gm Cumin (*jeera*) powder

METHOD

1 Boil the spinach in 6 cups water until
  tender. Remove, drain and mash with
  hands.

2 Heat the oil in a pressure cooker; add salt,
  asafoetida, and lamb with 1 cup water and
  pressure cook for 10 minutes. Add tomatoes
  and keep frying until the tomatoes are
  cooked.

3 Add the mashed spinach and keep stirring
  over high flame. Add red chilli powder,
  ginger powder, and cumin powder; mix
  well. Add ½ cup water and bring the
  mixture to the boil. Cook until the gravy is
  dry. Serve with rice or chapatti.

Gole al Syun

PUMPKIN COOKED WITH LAMB

Serves: 6

INGREDIENTS

1 kg / 2.2 lb Lamb, cut from leg, washed
1 kg / 2.2 lb Pumpkin (*kaddu*), peeled,
  washed, cut into medium-sized cubes
½ cup / 110 ml / 3½ fl oz Mustard /
  Refined oil
Salt to taste
¼ tsp Asafoetida (*hing*)
1 tsp / 3 gm Turmeric (*haldi*) powder
1 tsp / 3 gm Ginger powder (*sonth*)
2 tsp / 6 gm Fennel (*saunf*) powder
4 Dried red chillies (*sookhi lal mirch*)

METHOD

1 Heat the oil in a pressure cooker; add salt,
  asafoetida, and meat. Fry until the water is
  dried up. Add 1 cup water and pressure
  cook for 5 minutes.

2 Open the lid when the pressure drops and
  if meat is half tender, add pumpkin cubes
  and the spice powders. Pressure cook for
  5 minutes more. Remove the lid and
  transfer into a serving bowl.

3 Serve garnished with dried red chillies and
  enjoy with chapatti, rice or *nan*.

Kaliya
LAMB IN YELLOW GRAVY

Serves: 6

INGREDIENTS

1 kg / 2.2 lb
    Lamb, cut from
    shoulder and
    breast, washed
2 tbsp / 30 ml /
    1 fl oz Mustard
    / Refined oil
2 Cloves (*laung*)
2 Bay leaves (*tej patta*)
¼ tsp Asafoetida (*hing*)
2 tsp / 6 gm Turmeric (*haldi*) powder
2 tsp / 6 gm Ginger powder (*sonth*)
3 tsp / 9 gm Fennel (*saunf*) powder
Salt to taste
½ cup / 120 ml / 4 fl oz Milk
1 tsp / 3 gm Cumin (*jeera*) powder
1 tsp / 3 gm Black cardamoms (*badi elaichi*),
    coarsely ground
3 Green cardamoms (*choti elaichi*), crushed

METHOD

1 Heat the oil in a pressure cooker; add
  cloves, bay leaves, asafoetida, and meat. Fry
  for 10 minutes. Add 6 cups water, turmeric
  powder, ginger powder, fennel powder,
  and salt. Pressure cook for 5-10 minutes.

2 Remove the lid of the pressure cooker and
  check if the meat is tender. Add milk,
  cumin powder, black cardamom and green
  cardamom powder; bring to the boil.
  Simmer for 5 minutes.

3 Serve with rice.

Note: This is an excellent dish for the old and young.
Earlier, kaliya was cooked in a clay degchi for hours
over slow fire. Today, although a pressure cooker
is used, at traditional weddings it is still cooked in
degchis. This dish is still popular at Kashmiri
Pandit weddings.

Rogan Josh
LAMB IN RED GRAVY

Serves: 6

INGREDIENTS

1 kg / 2.2 lb Lamb,
    cut from leg,
    washed
1 cup / 220 ml /
    7 fl oz Mustard /
    Refined oil
Salt to taste
¼ tsp Asafoetida (*hing*)
2 Cinnamon (*dalchini*) sticks
2 Bay leaves (*tej patta*)
2 Cloves (*laung*)
1 tsp / 2 gm Cumin (*jeera*) seeds
3 tsp / 6 gm Red chilli powder
½ cup / 110 gm / 3½ oz Yoghurt (*dahi*)
2 tsp / 6 gm Ginger powder (*sonth*)
3 tsp / 9 gm Fennel (*saunf*) powder
3 Black cardamoms (*badi elaichi*), crushed
3 Green cardamoms (*choti elaichi*), crushed
1 tsp / 3 gm Cumin powder
¼ Saffron (*kesar*), optional

METHOD

1 Heat the oil in a vessel; add salt, asafoetida,
  cinnamon sticks, bay leaves, cloves, cumin
  seeds, and meat. Fry until the meat turns
  brown.

2 Add 1 cup water and red chilli powder; keep
  stirring with a ladle until the colour turns red.

3 Whisk yoghurt and add to the meat. Add
  2 cups water, ginger powder and fennel
  powder; cook until the meat is tender.

4 Add the cardamoms and cumin powder; mix
  well. Finally, add saffron if using. Simmer for
  2 minutes and serve with steamed rice.

Note: Cook in a pressure cooker, if in a hurry.
Personally I do not use a pressure cooker if the quality
of meat is good, as it gets tender while frying.

Gogji t, Syun
LAMB WITH TURNIPS

Serves: 6

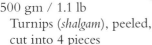

INGREDIENTS

1 kg / 2.2 lb
  Lamb, cut from
  breast and
  shoulder, washed
500 gm / 1.1 lb
  Turnips (*shalgam*), peeled,
  cut into 4 pieces
½ cup / 110 ml / 3½ fl oz Mustard oil
2 Cloves (*laung*)
Salt to taste
½ tsp Asafoetida (*hing*)
2 tsp / 6 gm Turmeric (*haldi*) powder
3 tsp / 9 gm Fennel (*saunf*) powder
2 tsp / 6 gm Ginger powder (*sonth*)

METHOD

1 Heat the oil in a pressure cooker; add cloves, meat, salt, and asafoetida. Keep frying for 10 minutes. Pour 6 cups water, turmeric powder, fennel powder, and ginger powder; mix well. Pressure cook for 5 minutes; remove from heat.

2 Heat 2 tbsp oil in a frying pan; fry the turnips 4-5 pieces at a time.

3 Remove the lid of the cooker, add the fried turnips and pressure cook again for 2 minutes. Remove from heat and let it cool down.

4 Remove the lid when the pressure drops and check if the meat is tender, if you find the gravy is thin then boil over high flame until the gravy thickens.

5 Serve hot.

Vost Haak t, Syun
GREEN / RED LEAVES WITH LAMB

Serves: 6

INGREDIENTS

1 kg / 2.2 lb Lamb,
  boneless, cut from
  leg, washed
500 gm / 1.1 lb *Vost
  haak*, sorted, washed,
  drained
1 cup / 220 ml / 7 fl oz Mustard /
  Refined oil
Salt to taste
½ tsp Asafoetida (*hing*)
2 Cloves (*laung*)
1 tsp / 2 gm Cumin (*jeera*) seeds
3 tsp / 9 gm Red chilli powder
2 tsp / 6 gm Ginger powder (*sonth*)
3 tsp / 9 gm Fennel (*saunf*) powder
1 cup / 225 gm / 8 oz Yoghurt (*dahi*),
  whisked
2 tsp / 6 gm Cumin (*jeera*) powder

METHOD

1 Heat the oil in a pressure cooker; add salt, asafoetida, cloves, cumin seeds, and lamb. Fry until the lamb is golden brown.

2 Add *vost haak*; mix well. Add red chilli powder, ginger powder, fennel powder, and 4 cups water; mix well with a ladle and pressure cook for 10 minutes.

3 Open the lid and check if the meat is tender. Add yoghurt and cook over high heat, stirring until the lamb and *vost haak* are really mixed well.

4 Serve hot.

Note: Vost haak *is a speciality of Kashmir. It is generally available in spring, the leaves are red or green. It is available in Delhi in winters from November onwards and if you do not get* vost haak *you can use* cholai ka sag *instead.*

The VVIP boat on the Jhelum River in the early 1900s.

Oluv t, Syun
POTATOES AND LAMB IN THICK GRAVY

Serves: 6

INGREDIENTS

1 kg / 2.2 lb Lamb, cut from leg
500 gm / 1.1 lb Potatoes, peeled, washed,
  cut into 4 long pieces
1 cup / 220 ml / 7 fl oz Mustard oil
2 Bay leaves (*tej patta*)
2 Cloves (*laung*)
1 Cinnamon (*dalchini*) stick
Salt to taste
3 tsp / 9 gm Red chilli powder
½ tsp Asafoetida (*hing*)
2 tsp / 6 gm Ginger powder (*sonth*)
3 tsp / 9 gm Fennel (*saunf*) powder
2 tsp / 6 gm Cumin (*jeera*) powder
3 Black cardamoms (*badi elaichi*), coarsely
  ground

METHOD

1 Heat the oil in a pan; fry the potatoes until
   they are perfect brown. Keep aside.

2 Reheat the same oil in a pressure cooker;
   add meat, bay leaves, cloves, cinnamon stick,
   and salt. Fry till the meat is golden brown.

3 Pour ½ cup water and red chilli powder;
   stir till the mixture turns red. Pour 6 cups
   water and all the spice powders. Pressure
   cook for 2 minutes. Remove the lid and
   check if the meat is tender. Then add fried
   potatoes and boil for 5-8 minutes. Add
   black cardamom powder and mix well.

4 Serve hot with steamed rice or chapatti.

Champ
LAMB CHOPS

Serves: 6

INGREDIENTS

1 kg / 2.2 lb Lamb chops, flattened nicely
1 cup / 225 gm / 8 oz Yoghurt (*dahi*)
2 tsp / 6 gm Ginger (*adrak*) paste, fresh
2 tsp / 6 gm Garlic (*lasan*) paste
Salt to taste
1 tbsp / 15 ml Lemon (*nimbu*) juice
2 tsp / 10 gm Papaya paste
3 tbsp / 45 ml / 1½ fl oz Refined oil
  for mixing
1 tsp / 5 ml Wine vinegar
2 tsp / 6 gm Red chilli powder
2 tsp / 6 gm Cumin (*jeera*) powder
1 cup / 220 ml / 7 fl oz Refined oil for frying

METHOD

1 Mix the lamb chops, yoghurt, ginger paste,
   garlic paste, salt, lemon juice, papaya paste,
   oil, vinegar, red chilli powder, and cumin
   powder together in a bowl. Marinate for
   12 hours.

2 Heat the oil in a frying pan; fry the chops
   until golden brown. Alternatively preheat
   oven to 180°C / 350°F and grill.

3 Serve hot with *nan* or chapatti or rice pulao.

*Note: When buying lamb chops make sure you get
them chopped nicely. They should be flatted nicely.*

Bukvetch Chagil t, Charvan

SPICY KIDNEYS, TESTES AND LIVER

Serves: 6

INGREDIENTS

1 kg / 2.2 lb Lamb liver, testes, kidney
   washed and cut into 4 pieces, removing fat
   from kidney
1 cup / 220 ml / 7 fl oz Mustard /
   Refined oil
2 Cloves (*laung*)
Salt to taste
½ tsp Asafoetida (*hing*)
3 tsp / 9 gm Red chilli powder
2 tsp / 6 gm Ginger powder (*sonth*)
1 tsp / 3 gm Turmeric (*haldi*) powder
2 tsp / 6 gm Fennel (*saunf*) powder
1 tsp / 3 gm Cumin (*jeera*) powder

METHOD

1 Heat the oil in a frying pan; add cloves,
   salt, asafoetida, liver and kidneys. Fry till
   golden brown. Add red chilli powder and
   ½ cup water; mix well. Add all the spice
   powders and 2 cups water. Cook until the
   liver is tender.

2 In a separate pot, boil the testes in 2 cups
   water with ½ tsp turmeric powder and
   ½ tsp salt for 3 minutes. Drain and add to
   the liver. Bring to the boil and serve with
   rice, chapatti, *nan* or tandoori roti.

Tchokh Charvan

TANGY LIVER

Serves: 6

INGREDIENTS

1 kg / 2.2 lb Liver, cut into small cubes,
   1 cm long x ½ cm wide
½ cup / 110 ml / 3½ fl oz Mustard oil
2 Cloves (*laung*)
¼ tsp Asafoetida (*hing*)
3 tsp / 9 gm Red chilli powder
2 tsp / 6 gm Ginger powder (*sonth*)
2 tsp / 6 gm Fennel (*saunf*) powder
1 tsp / 3 gm Turmeric (*haldi*) powder
½ cup / 100 ml / 3½ fl oz Tamarind (*imli*)
   liquid
1 tsp / 3 gm Cumin (*jeera*) powder
Salt to taste

METHOD

1 Heat the oil in a pot; add cloves, asafoetida,
   and liver. Fry till brown. Pour 2 cups water,
   red chilli powder, ginger powder, fennel
   powder, turmeric powder, and salt; cook
   for 10 minutes.

2 Add tamarind liquid and boil for 5 minutes.
   Reduce heat and simmer for 5 minutes.
   Add cumin powder; mix well.

3 Serve hot with rice.

Through the blooming mustard fields near Srinagar.
Photograph: Mukhtar Ahmad

Pachh Rogan Josh

TROTTER IN RED GRAVY

Serves: 6

INGREDIENTS

12 Trotters, cleaned, trimmed and washed in hot water
2 cups / 440 ml / 15 fl oz Mustard oil
½ tsp Asafoetida (*hing*)
Salt to taste
1 tsp / 2 gm Cumin (*jeera*) seeds
2 Cloves (*laung*)
2 Cinnamon (*dalchini*) sticks
1 tsp / 2 gm Red chilli powder
3 tsp / 9 gm Fennel (*saunf*) powder
2 tsp / 6 gm Ginger powder (*sonth*)
2 tsp / 6 gm Cumin (*jeera*) powder
2 Green cardamoms (*choti elaichi*), crushed
2 Black cardamoms (*badi elaichi*), crushed

METHOD

1 Heat the oil a pressure cooker; add asafoetida, salt, cumin seeds, cloves, cinnamon sticks, and trotters. Fry until golden brown. Add red chilli powder and 6 cups water; mix. And rest of the spice powders.

2 Pressure cook for 30 minutes. Open the lid when the pressure drops and check if the trotters are tender, if not pressure cook again for 15 minutes and keep checking till they are tender.

3 Add crushed green and black cardamoms; cook until oil separates.

4 Serve hot with steamed rice.

Pachh Ras

TROTTER SOUP

Serves: 6

INGREDIENTS

10 Sheep knuckles, washed in hot water
2 tbsp / 30 ml / 1 fl oz Mustard oil
¼ tsp Asafoetida (*hing*)
3 tsp / 9 gm Fennel (*saunf*) powder
2 tsp / 6 gm Ginger powder (*sonth*)
2 tsp / 6 gm Turmeric (*haldi*) powder
2 Black cardamoms (*badi elaichi*)
Salt to taste

METHOD

1 Cook the knuckles in a pressure cooker with 20 cups water and all the spices for about 30 minutes.

2 Remove the lid when the pressure drops and check if they are tender. If not, cook for some more time till they are tender.

3 You can remove the knuckles and serve the soup only, or enjoy the whole dish with steamed rice.

Note: In olden times this soup was cooked in handies on slow heat the whole day. Today we can use a pressure cooker. So enjoy the soup which is an excellent source of calcium. Get knuckles trimmed and cleaned from the butcher.

A shikara ride in the pristine Dal Lake.
Photograph: Wajid Dabru

Chicken & Fish

Gaad t, Tamater
FISH IN TOMATO GRAVY

Serves: 6

INGREDIENTS

1 kg / 2.2 lb Fish (*Singhara/Salmon/Rohu*),
  cleaned, trimmed, cut into 2″-thick
  round pieces
1 cup Tomatoes, chopped
½ tsp / 1½ gm Turmeric (*haldi*) powder
1 cup / 220 ml / 7 fl oz Mustard oil
  for frying
Salt to taste
½ tsp Asafoetida (*hing*)
2 Cloves (*laung*)
2 tsp / 6 gm Red chilli powder
2 tsp / 6 gm Fennel (*saunf*) powder
2 tsp / 6 gm Ginger powder (*sonth*)
1 tsp / 3 gm *Ver* masala (see p. 16)

METHOD

1 Wash fish and drain in a holed basket.
   Sprinkle turmeric powder all over.

2 Heat the oil in a frying pan; sprinkle a pinch
   of salt over the fish to avoid splattering. Fry
   the fish until brown, turning it once or
   twice, over high heat.

3 Take the leftover oil in a separate vessel;
   add asafoetida, cloves, and tomatoes. Pour
   ½ cup water and make a paste.

4 Add all the spices with 4 cups water. Bring
   to the boil. Add fried fish and cook until
   the gravy thickens.

5 Serve with steamed rice.

Gaad t, Nadir
FISH COOKED WITH LOTUS STEMS

Serves: 6

INGREDIENTS

1 kg / 2.2 lb Fish, cleaned, trimmed, cut
  into cubes
500 gm / 1.1 lb Lotus stems (*kamal kakri*),
  washed, cut into 3 cm pieces
1 tsp / 3 gm Turmeric (*haldi*) powder
1 cup / 220 ml / 7 fl oz Mustard oil
½ tsp Asafoetida (*hing*) liquid (see p. 17)
Salt to taste
3 tsp / 9 gm Red chilli powder
2 Cloves (*laung*)
3 tsp / 9 gm Fennel (*saunf*) powder
2 tsp / 6 gm Ginger powder (*sonth*)
2 tbsp / 30 ml / 1 fl oz Tamarind (*imli*)
  liquid or
2 tbsp / 10 ml Lemon (*nimbu*) juice
2 tsp / 6 gm *Ver* masala (see p. 16)

METHOD

1 Wash the fish, drain and sprinkle turmeric
   powder all over.

2 Heat the oil in a frying pan; fry the lotus
   stems until light brown. Keep aside.

3 Fry the fish in the same oil until golden
   brown.

4 Take the same oil in another vessel; add,
   asafoetida liquid, salt, red chilli powder,
   cloves, and 2 cups water. Bring to the boil
   and stir until the mixture turns red. Add 4
   more cups of water, fennel powder, ginger
   powder, fried fish, and lotus stems; cook
   for 10-15 minutes. Add
   ¼ cup tamarind
   liquid or lemon
   juice and *ver*
   masala; cook for
   5 more minutes.

5 Serve hot with
   steamed rice.

Gaad t, Munj

FISH COOKED WITH KNOL KHOL

Serves: 6

INGREDIENTS

1 kg / 2.2 lb Fish (*Singhara/Salmon/Rohu*),
  cleaned, trimmed, cut into 2″-thick
  round pieces
500 gm / 1.1 lb Knol khol (*kholrabi*), peeled,
  cut into 2″-thick round pieces
1 tsp / 3 gm Turmeric (*haldi*) powder
1 cup / 220 ml / 7 fl oz Mustard oil
2 Cloves (*laung*)
½ tsp Asafoetida (*hing*) liquid (see p. 17)
3 tsp / 9 gm Red chilli powder
Salt to taste
2 tsp / 6 gm Ginger powder (*sonth*)
3 tsp / 9 gm Fennel (*saunf*) powder
2 tsp / 6 gm *Ver* masala (see p. 16)

METHOD

1 Wash the fish, sprinkle turmeric powder
   and keep aside to drain in a big holed basket.

2 Heat the oil in a frying pan; fry the fish till
   golden brown.

3 Fry knol khol in the same oil till golden
   brown.

4 Take the same oil in another vessel; add
   cloves, asafoetida liquid, red chilli powder,
   salt, ginger powder, and fennel powder.
   Add 4 cups water and bring to the boil.
   Add fried fish and knol khol; cook till the
   gravy thickens and fish is tender.

5 Sprinkle
   ver masala and
   cook for a
   minute.
   Serve with
   steamed rice.

Gaad t, Muj

FISH COOKED WITH RADISH

Serves: 6

INGREDIENTS

1 kg / 2.2 lb Fish
  (*Singhara/Salmon/Rohu*),
  cleaned, trimmed, cut into
  2″-thick, round pieces
500 gm / 1.1 lb Radish (*shalgam*), peeled,
  washed, cut into 2″-thick round pieces
1 cup / 220 ml / 7 fl oz Mustard oil
Salt to taste
½ tsp Asafoetida (*hing*)
3 tsp / 9 gm Red chilli powder
3 tsp / 9 gm Fennel (*saunf*) powder
2 tsp / 6 gm Ginger powder (*sonth*)
1 tsp / 3 gm Turmeric (*haldi*) powder
2 tsp / 6 gm *Ver* masala (see p. 16)
¼ cup / 50 ml / 1¾ fl oz Tamarind (*imli*)
  liquid
3 tbsp / 45 ml / 1½ fl oz Lemon (*nimbu*)
  juice

METHOD

1 Wash and drain the fish. Sprinkle turmeric
   powder over the fish.

2 Heat the oil in a frying pan; fry the fish
   golden brown. Keep aside. Fry the radish in
   the same oil and keep aside.

3 Take the leftover oil in a deep vessel; add
   salt, asafoetida, red chilli powder, 6 cups
   water, add all the spice powders; bring to
   the boil. Add fish and radish and cook till
   the gravy thickens.

4 Lastly pour the tamarind liquid or lemon
   juice and boil for a minute.

5 Serve with steamed rice.

One of the most unique features of Srinagar was the prevalence of wooden architecture. Seen here is a bridge made of deodar on the river Jhelum.

Gaad t, Choont
FISH COOKED WITH GREEN APPLES

Serves: 6

INGREDIENTS

1 kg / 2.2 lb Fish
(*Singhara/Salmon/
Rohu*), cleaned, trimmed, cut into 2″-thick,
round pieces
500 gm / 1.1 lb Cooking green apples, cut
into 4 pieces each
1 tsp / 3 gm Turmeric (*haldi*) powder
1 cup / 220 ml / 7 fl oz Mustard oil
2 Cloves (*laung*)
½ tsp Asafoetida (*hing*)
3 tsp / 9 gm Red chilli powder
2 tsp / 6 gm Ginger powder (*sonth*)
2 tsp / 6 gm Fennel (*saunf*) powder
Salt to taste
4 Green chillies

METHOD

1 Wash and drain the fish. Sprinkle turmeric
powder and keep aside for some time until
the water is drained out.

2 Heat the oil in a pan; fry the fish until
golden brown.

3 Fry the apples in the same oil turning once;
remove and keep aside.

4 Take the leftover oil in a separate pan; add
cloves, asafoetida, red chilli powder, 6 cups
water and rest of the spice powders. Add
fish and cook for 10 minutes. Add fried
apples and cook for another 5 minutes.

5 Serve hot garnished with green chillies and
accompanied with rice.

Gaad t, Aar
FISH COOKED WITH PLUM

Serves: 6

INGREDIENTS

1 kg / 2.2 lb Fish (*Singhara/Salmon/Rohu*),
cleaned, trimmed, cut into 2-thick, round
pieces
500 gm / 1.1 lb Raw plum, washed, pat
dried, pricked with a knife
1 tsp / 3 gm Turmeric (*haldi*) powder
1 cup / 220 ml / 7 oz Mustard oil
Salt to taste
½ tsp Asafoetida (*hing*)
3 tsp / 9 gm Red chilli powder
2 tsp / 6 gm Ginger powder (*sonth*)
2 tsp / 6 gm Fennel (*saunf*) powder

METHOD

1 Wash the fish and drain in a holed basket.
Sprinkle turmeric powder all over the fish.

2 Heat the oil in a frying pan; add a little bit
of salt and fry the fish till golden brown.

3 Take the leftover oil in a large vessel; add
asafoetida, salt, 6 cups water, red chilli
powder, and rest of the spice powders;
bring to the boil. Add fish and cook for 15
minutes. Add plum and cook for 5 minutes
on high heat.

4 Serve hot with steamed rice.

Haak t, Thool
GREENS WITH EGGS

Serves: 6

INGREDIENTS

10 Eggs, hard-boiled, shelled
500 gm / 1.1 lb Kashmiri greens (*haak*),
   cleaned, washed
1 cup / 220 ml / 7 fl oz Mustard oil for frying
½ tsp Asafoetida (*hing*)
Salt to taste
3 tsp / 9 gm Red chilli powder
2 tsp / 6 gm Ginger powder (*sonth*)
5 Dried red chillies (*sookhi lal mirch*), deseeded
2 tsp / 6 gm *Ver* masala (see p. 16)

METHOD

1 Prick the eggs with a tooth pick and keep
   aside.

2 Heat the oil in a deep pan; fry the eggs, 4-5
   at a time, till light brown.

3 Take the leftover oil in a pressure cooker;
   add asafoetida, salt, red chilli powder, ginger
   powder, 6 cups water, eggs, and greens.
   Pressure cook for 10 minutes or till 2
   whistles. Remove from heat.

4 Open the lid when the pressure drops. Add
   dried red chillies and *ver* masala. Return to
   heat and cook over high heat, until the
   gravy thickens.

5 Serve hot with rice or chapatti.

HoGaad t, Haak
DRIED FISH COOKED WITH GREENS

Serves: 6

INGREDIENTS

250 gm / 9 oz Dried fish, skin scraped, fins
   removed, soaked for 5 minutes
200 gm / 7 oz Kashmiri spinach (*haak*),
   cleaned, washed
½ cup / 110 ml / 3½ fl oz Mustard oil
½ tsp Asafoetida (*hing*)
2 tsp / 6 gm Red chilli powder
1 tsp / 3 gm Ginger powder (*sonth*)
1 tsp / 3 gm Turmeric (*haldi*) powder
1 tsp / 3 gm Fennel (*saunf*) powder
Salt to taste
4 Dried red chillies (*sookhi lal mirch*), deseeded
1 tsp / 3 gm *Ver* masala (see p. 16)

METHOD

1 Scrape the fish skin again and wash until
   really clean. Drain. Cut into 4 pieces if they
   are large and if small leave the fish whole.

2 Heat the oil in a deep pot; add asafoetida,
   salt, and fish. Fry until dark brown (do not
   burn). Add red chilli powder, 4 cups water,
   ginger powder, turmeric powder, and fennel
   powder; bring to the boil.

3 Add *haak* and cook until the fish and greens
   are tender. Add dried red chillies and *ver*
   masala; cook for 2 minutes. Serve hot.

*Note: Dried fish is available in
Srinagar. Small fish called
sardine is sun-dried in
summer to be used in
winters. This
sun-dried fish is
called* Raz hogard.
*The larger ones are
cleaned after slitting
their stomachs and
are called* Pach
hogard.

*A view of the snow-capped mountains
and the blooming mustard field.
Photograph: S. Irfan*

Top: A papier maché worker.
Bottom: Quiet waters: serene and beautiful!

VEGETARIAN

75 SOUCHAL T NADIR
Greens with fried lotus stems

78 TAMATAR T, NADIR
Lotus stems cooked with tomatoes

79 TCHOK NADIR
Lotus stems in sour gravy

79 VOST HAAK T NADIR
Red coloured greens with lotus stems

80 NADIR YAKHNI
Lotus stems in yoghurt

81 WANGEN YAKHNI
Fried aubergine in yoghurt

82 RAZMA HEMB T, WANGEN
French beans with aubergine

82 TCHONT T WANGEN
Cooking apples with aubergine

83 SOUCHAL T WANGEN
Kashmiri spinach with aubergine

83 TAMATER T, WANGEN
Tomatoes with aubergine

86 TCHOK WANGEN
Tangy aubergine

86 AL ROGAN JOSH
Pumpkin in red gravy

87 AL YAKHNI
Bottle gourd in yoghurt

88 KANGUCH YAKHNI
Mushrooms in yoghurt sauce

88 PHOOL ROGAN JOSH
Cauliflower in thick red gravy

89 KANGUCH T, CHAMAN
Mushrooms and cottage cheese in yoghurt

89 CHAMAN T MEETH
Cottage cheese in fenugreek sauce

91 CHAMAN KALIYA
Cottage cheese in yellow gravy

92 WANGEN HETCH, TAMBER LAGITH
Dried aubergine in tamarind sauce

92 AL HETCH IN ZAMUDUD
Dried bottle gourd in yoghurt

93 HAAK T CHAMAN
Kashmiri spinach with cottage cheese

93 THOOL RAZMA YAKHNI
Green kidney beans in yoghurt

94 KAREL T WANGEN DUED LAGITH
Bitter gourd and aubergine in yoghurt

95 GURDOL T, OLUV
Raw plum with potatoes

95 VERIFOL T, OLUV
Sun-dried black lentils with potatoes

96 AL KANEJ T, WANGEN
Pumpkin greens with aubergine

96 MUJ PATTAR T, WANGEN
Radish leaves with aubergine

Munj Haak

KNOL KHOL FLAVOURED WITH ASAFOETIDA

Serves: 6

INGREDIENTS

1 kg / 2.2 lb Knol khol (*kholrabi*) with leaves,
  medium-sized, peeled
½ cup / 110 ml / 3½ fl oz Mustard oil
Salt to taste
½ tsp Asafoetida (*hing*)
6 Dried red chillies (*sookhi lal mirch*)

METHOD

1 Sort out the green leaves and cut the
   stems out. Shred the peeled balls into fine
   slices. Wash the leaves and knol khol slices
   together in a large vessel.

2 Heat the oil in a pressure cooker; add salt and
   asafoetida. Add sliced knol khol and leaves.
   Pour 1 cup water, stirring well with a ladle.
   Pressure cook over high heat for 15 minutes
   or till 3 whistles. Remove the lid of cooker
   under running tap water immediately.

3 Put the cooker over high heat again and
   cook the knol khol until the water dries up.
   Pour 3 cups water and dried red chillies.
   Bring to the boil for 5 minutes.

4 Serve with steamed rice.

Dum Munj

FRIED KNOL KHOL IN YOGHURT

Serves: 6

INGREDIENTS

1 kg / 2.2 lb Knol khol (*kholrabi*), peeled, washed,
  cut into 2 cm-thick round pieces
1 cup / 220 ml / 7 fl oz Mustard oil for frying
½ tsp Asafoetida (*hing*)
2 Cloves (*laung*)
Salt to taste
3 tsp / 6 gm Red chilli powder
2 tbsp / 30 gm / 1 oz Yoghurt (*dahi*), whisked
1 tsp / 3 gm Ginger powder (*sonth*)
2 tsp / 6 gm Fennel (*saunf*) powder
1 tsp / 3 gm *Ver* masala (see p. 16)

METHOD

1 Heat the oil in a pan; fry the knol khol
   until golden brown.

2 In a separate vessel, take 3 tbsp oil from
   the pan. Add asafoetida, cloves, salt, 3 cups
   water, red chilli powder, yoghurt, ginger
   powder, and fennel powder; bring to the
   boil. Add fried knol kohl and mix well.

3 Cook for 10 minutes. Add *ver* masala and
   cook till the knol khol is tender and the
   gravy is thick.

4 Serve hot with steamed rice.

Dum Oluv
WHOLE SPICY POTATOES

Serves: 6

INGREDIENTS

1 kg / 2.2 lb Potatoes, round, medium-sized
2 cups / 440 ml / 15 fl oz Mustard /
  Refined oil for frying
2 Bay leaves (*tej patta*)
2 Cloves (*laung*)
1 tsp / 2 gm Cumin (*jeera*) seeds
1 Cinnamon (*dalchini*) stick
3 tsp / 6 gm Red chilli powder
Salt to taste
½ cup / 110 gm / 3½ oz Yoghurt (*dahi*)
1 tsp / 3 gm Ginger powder (*sonth*)
2 tsp / 6 gm Fennel (*saunf*) powder
1 tsp / 3 gm Black cardamom (*badi elaichi*) powder
1 tsp / 2½ gm Black cumin (*shah jeera*) seeds

METHOD

1 Boil the potatoes till tender. Peel the skin and prick the potatoes deep with a tooth pick or a fork.

2 Heat the oil in a deep pan; deep-fry the potatoes until golden brown.

3 Take the leftover oil in a separate vessel; add bay leaves, cloves, cumin seeds, cinnamon stick, red chilli powder, and salt. Add ½ cup water. Keep stirring until the mixture turns red. Whisk the yoghurt in a bowl and add to the gravy. Add 4 cups water, ginger powder, fennel powder, and cumin powder; mix well.

4 Add the fried potatoes to the gravy and boil over medium heat for 15 minutes. Simmer for another 15 minutes.

5 Add black cardamom powder and black cumin seeds; mix well. Serve with steamed rice or *nan*.

Autumn in the Mughal Gardens, Srinagar. Photograph: Mukhtar Ahmad

Haak

LEAFY GREENS

Serves: 6

INGREDIENTS

1 kg / 2.2 lb Kashmiri Spinach (*haak*)
1 cup / 220 ml / 7 fl oz Mustard oil
½ tsp Asafoetida (*hing*)
Salt to taste
5 Dried red chillies (*sookhi lal mirch*)

METHOD

1 Wash the green leaves and drain in a holed basket.

2 Heat the oil in a pressure cooker; add asafoetida and salt. Pour 6 cups water and bring to the boil. Add the leaves and keep stirring for a few minutes. Pressure cook for 10 minutes. Remove the lid under running tap water to retain the green colour.

3 Add dried red chillies and cook for 2 minutes.

4 Serve hot with steamed rice.

Note: Haak is the main green leafy vegetable in a Kashmiri meal. If haak is not available cook spinach the same way.

Haak t, Nadir

GREENS WITH LOTUS STEMS

Serves: 6

INGREDIENTS

1 kg / 2.2 lb Kashmiri Spinach (*haak*), sort, stems chopped, washed
250 gm / 9 oz Lotus stems (*kamal kakri*), scraped, cut crosswise 2″ long
1 cup / 220 ml / 7 fl oz Mustard oil
Salt to taste
½ tsp Asafoetida (*hing*)
5 Dried red chillies (*sookhi lal mirch*)

METHOD

1 Heat the oil in a pressure cooker; add salt, asafoetida, and lotus stems. Fry for 5 minutes. Add 6 cups water and bring to the boil. Add greens and stir well. Pressure cook for 10 minutes.

2 Remove the lid under running water tap. Add dried red chillies and bring to the boil for 2 minutes.

3 Serve hot with steamed rice and yoghurt.

Note: This vegetarian dish is best served as an accompaniment to Rogan josh.

Moung Dal t, Nadir

GREEN GRAM LENTIL WITH LOTUS STEMS

Serves: 6

INGREDIENTS

500 gm / 1.1 lb Green gram whole (*moong*),
  soaked in warm water for 1 hour
250 gm / 9 oz Lotus stems (*kamal kakri*),
  washed, cut into 3 cm-long pieces
Salt to taste
1½ tsp / 4½ gm Turmeric (*haldi*) powder
1 tbsp / 15 ml Mustard oil
½ tsp Asafoetida (*hing*)
3 tsp / 9 gm Fennel (*saunf*) powder
1½ tsp / 4½ gm Ginger powder (*sonth*)
5 Dried red or green chillies

METHOD

1 Pressure cook the lentil and lotus stems
  with salt, turmeric powder and 4 cups
  water for 10 minutes.

2 Heat the oil in a separate pan; add
  asafoetida, fennel powder, and ginger
  powder; stir. Add this to the lentil mixture
  in the pressure cooker and simmer for
  5 minutes.

3 Serve hot garnished with dried red or
  green chillies.

Gogje t, Nadir

TURNIPS WITH LOTUS STEMS

Serves: 6

INGREDIENTS

1 kg / 2.2 lb Turnips (*shalgam*), peeled, cut
  crosswise, washed, drained
500 gm / 1.1 lb Lotus stems (*kamal kakri*),
  cleaned, cut crosswise, washed, drained
2 tbsp / 30 ml / 1 fl oz Mustard /
  Refined oil
Salt to taste
½ tsp Asafoetida (*hing*)
4 Dried red or green chillies
½ tsp *Ver* masala (see p. 16)

METHOD

1 Heat the oil in a pressure cooker; add salt,
  asafoetida, turnips, and lotus stems. Fry till
  the water dries up. Add 4 cups water and
  pressure cook for 5 minutes.

2 Remove the lid under running tap water
  and add dried red or green chillies. Bring
  to the boil till the gravy thickens. Sprinkle
  ver masala and serve hot.

3 This unique combination of vegetables can
  be enjoyed with steamed rice.

Razma t, Gogje

KIDNEY BEANS WITH TURNIPS

Serves: 6

INGREDIENTS

1 kg / 2.2 lb Kidney beans (*rajma*), soaked
overnight, drained
1 kg / 2.2 lb Turnip (*shalgam*), peeled, cut
into 4-6 pieces
Salt to taste
2 tsp / 6 gm Ginger powder (*sonth*)
3 tsp / 9 gm Red chilli powder
½ tsp Asafoetida (*hing*)
2 tbsp / 30 ml / 1 fl oz Mustard / Refined oil
2 tsp / 6 gm *Ver* masala (see p. 16)

METHOD

1 Put the soaked beans in a pressure cooker.
Add 12 cups water, salt, 2 tsp ginger
powder, red chilli powder, and asafoetida.
Pressure cook for 5 minutes or till one
whistle. Remove the lid of the cooker and
keep aside.

2 Heat the oil in a frying pan; fry the turnips
for 5 minutes.

3 Add the turnips to the kidney beans in the
pressure cooker and cook with out pressure
until the turnip gets cooked. Add *ver* masala
and bring to the boil.

4 Serve with steamed rice.

*Note: This dish always tastes better if cooked the
previous day.*

Palak t, Nadir

MASHED SPINACH WITH LOTUS STEMS

Serves: 6

INGREDIENTS

1 kg / 2.2 lb Spinach (*palak*), discard stems,
leaves washed
1 Lotus stem (*kamal kakri*), medium-sized,
cleaned, cut into round 1 cm-thick pieces
½ cup / 110 ml / 3½ fl oz Mustard /
Refined oil
½ tsp Asafoetida (*hing*)
Salt to taste
500 gm / 1.1 lb Tomatoes, chopped
2 tsp / 1½ gm Red chilli powder
1 tsp / 3 gm Ginger powder (*sonth*)
1 tsp / 3 gm *Ver* masala (see p. 16)

METHOD

1 Boil the spinach; keep stirring occasionally
till tender. Drain the water in a strainer and
keep the spinach aside. When cool, mash
the spinach with clean hands.

2 Heat the oil in a vessel; fry the lotus stem
till golden brown. Remove and keep aside.
Add asafoetida, salt, and tomatoes; stir with
a ladle to a smooth paste.

3 Add the mashed spinach, red chilli
powder, and ginger powder; keep stirring
till it is mixed well. Add ½ cup water and
fried lotus stem; cook till the water dries
up. Add *ver* masala
and mix well.

4 Serve hot
with
steamed
rice or
chapatti.

Razma Hemb t Nadir

SPICY FRENCH BEANS WITH LOTUS STEMS

Serves: 6

INGREDIENTS

1 kg / 2.2 lb French beans, washed, cut into
  2″ pieces
250 gm / 9 oz Lotus stems (*kamal kakri*),
  peeled, cut into 1 cm-thick round slices
2 tbsp / 30 ml / 1 fl oz Refined oil
1 tsp / 2 gm Cumin (*jeera*) seeds
Salt to taste
2 tsp / 6 gm Red chilli powder
1 tsp / 3 gm Ginger powder (*sonth*)
3-4 Dried red chillies (*sookhi lal mirch*)

METHOD

1 Heat the oil in a frying pan; add French
  beans, lotus stems, cumin seeds, and salt.
  Cook on high heat for 10 minutes. Add
  red chilli powder and ginger powder; mix
  well. Simmer till the beans are tender.

2 Add dried red chillies and serve hot with
  chapatti, steamed rice or any dish of your
  choice.

Souchal t, Nadir

GREENS WITH FRIED LOTUS STEMS

Serves: 6

INGREDIENTS

1 kg / 2.2 lb Kashmiri *souchal*, sort out the
  leaves, discard the hard stems
250 gm / 9 oz Lotus stems (*kamal kakri*),
  washed, drained, cut into 1 cm-thick pieces
½ cup / 110 ml / 3½ fl oz Mustard oil
Salt to taste
½ tsp Asafoetida (*hing*)
2 tsp / 6 gm Red chilli powder
1 tsp / 3 gm *Ver* masala (see p. 16)
4 Dried red chillies (*sookhi lal mirch*)

METHOD

1 Fry the lotus stems in hot oil till golden
  brown. Remove and keep aside.

2 Take some oil in a pan; add salt, asafoetida,
  and *souchal*. Keep stirring on high heat till
  the water is absorbed. Add the fried lotus
  stems and mix well with a ladle.

3 Add red chilli powder and keep stirring till
  it dries. Sprinkle *ver* masala and mix well.

4 Serve garnished with dried red chillies
  and accompanied with steamed rice or *nan*
  or chapatti.

A gathering of women in their traditional outfits in the early 1900s.

Tamatar t, Nadir

LOTUS STEMS COOKED WITH TOMATOES

Serves: 6

INGREDIENTS

1 kg / 2.2 lb Lotus stems (*kamal kakri*), scraped, cut into 2″-long pieces, washed thoroughly
700 gm / 25 oz Tomatoes, chopped
½ cup / 110 ml / 3½ fl oz Mustard / Refined oil
Salt to taste
3 tsp / 9 gm Red chilli powder
2 tsp / 6 gm Ginger powder (*sonth*)
1 tsp / 3 gm Cumin (*jeera*) powder
2 tsp / 6 gm Fennel (*saunf*) powder

METHOD

1 Heat the mustard oil in a pressure cooker till smoking; fry the lotus stems for 5-10 minutes. Add tomatoes and stir with a ladle. Add salt and cook until the mixture becomes dry.

2 Add red chilli powder, ginger powder, cumin powder, fennel powder and 3 cups water. Pressure cook for 5 minutes. Remove the lid and simmer for 5 minutes.

3 Serve hot with steamed rice, *nan* or chapatti.

Top: Navigating in the backwaters during winter.
Below: Heavy burden! Carrying hay long ago.

78

Tchok Nadir

LOTUS STEMS IN SOUR GRAVY

Serves: 6

INGREDIENTS

1 kg / 2.2 lb Lotus stems (*kamal kakri*),
  scraped, cut into 2″-long pieces, washed
  thoroughly
½ cup / 110 ml / 3½ fl oz Mustard /
  Refined oil
½ tsp Asafoetida (*hing*)
Salt to taste
1 tsp / 2 gm Cumin (*jeera*) seeds
3 tsp / 9 gm Red chilli powder
2 tsp / 6 gm Ginger powder (*sonth*)
3 tsp / 9 gm Fennel (*saunf*) powder
½ cup / 100 ml / 3½ fl oz Tamarind liquid

METHOD

1 Heat the oil in a pressure cooker; add
  asafoetida, salt, cumin seeds, and lotus
  stems. Fry for 10 minutes.

2 Add red chilli powder, ginger powder,
  fennel powder, and 3 cups water; stir and
  pressure cook for 5 minutes. Remove the
  lid and add tamarind liquid; cook until the
  gravy thickens.

3 Serve hot accompanied with any kind of dal
  or greens *(haak)*.

Vost Haak t, Nadir

RED COLOURED GREENS WITH LOTUS STEMS

Serves: 6

INGREDIENTS

1 kg / 2.2 lb Red greens (*vost haak*), leaves
  sorted, drained
200 gm / 7 oz Lotus stems (*kamal kakri*),
  washed, cut into small round pieces
½ cup / 110 ml / 3½ oz Mustard oil
½ tsp Asafoetida (*hing*)
Salt to taste
3 tsp / 9 gm Red chilli powder
2 tsp / 6 gm Ginger powder (*sonth*)
½ cup / 110 gm / 3½ oz Yoghurt (*dahi*),
  whisked
1 tsp / 3 gm *Ver* masala (see p. 16)

METHOD

1 Heat the oil in a pressure cooker; add
  asafoetida, salt, and *vost haak*. Mix well with
  a ladle and pressure cook for 10 minutes.
  Open the lid and cook on high heat.

2 Stir-fry the lotus stems in another pan.
  Remove and add to the cooker along with
  red chilli powder, ginger powder, and
  yoghurt; mix well until the gravy thickens.

3 Add *ver* masala, mix well and simmer for
  5 minutes.

4 Serve with steamed rice or anything of
  your choice.

Nadir Yakhni

LOTUS STEMS IN YOGHURT

Serves: 6

INGREDIENTS

1 kg / 2.2 lb Lotus stems (*kamal kakri*), scraped, washed, cut into 1″-long pieces
3 cups / 675 gm / 24 oz Yoghurt (*dahi*), whisked
½ cup / 110 ml / 3½ fl oz Mustard / Refined oil
2 Bay leaves (*tej patta*)
2 Cinnamon (*dalchini*) sticks
2 Cloves (*laung*)
3 tsp / 9 gm Fennel (*saunf*) powder
2 tsp / 6 gm Ginger powder (*sonth*)
Salt to taste
3 tsp / 9 gm Black cumin (*shah jeera*) seeds
3 Black cardamoms (*badi elaichi*), crushed
4 Green cardamoms (*choti elaichi*), crushed
1 tsp / 5 gm Cornflour

METHOD

1 Heat the oil in a pressure cooker; add bay leaves, cinnamon sticks, cloves, 6 cups water, fennel powder, ginger powder, and salt. Mix well.

2 Add lotus stems and pressure cook for 5 minutes. Remove the lid of the cooker and boil on high heat for 10 minutes or until the lotus stems are tender.

3 Add whisked yoghurt and black cumin seeds; mix well with a ladle and keep stirring. Add crushed black and green cardamom.

4 Mix the cornflour with 2 tsp water and pour into pressure cooker. Boil for 2 minutes and simmer for 2 minutes.

5 Serve with steamed rice and *dum oluv* (see p. 71).

A quick smoke in autumn.
Photograph: Mukhtar Ahmad

Wangen Yakhni

FRIED AUBERGINE IN YOGHURT

Serves: 6

INGREDIENTS

1 kg / 2.2 lb Aubergine (*baigan*), washed, cut into 4 pieces
2 cups / 450 gm / 1 lb Yoghurt (*dahi*), whisked
2 cups / 440 ml / 15 fl oz Refined oil for frying
Salt to taste
1 Bay leaf (*tej patta*)
2 tsp / 4 gm Cumin (*jeera*) seeds
1 Cinnamon (*dalchini*) stick
3 Cloves (*laung*)
3 tsp / 9 gm Fennel (*saunf*) powder
2 tsp / 6 gm Ginger powder (*sonth*)
1 tsp / 3 gm Cumin (*jeera*) powder
1 tsp / 2½ gm Black cumin (*shah jeera*) seeds
2 Green cardamoms (*choti elaichi*), coarsely ground
5 Green chillies, large ones

METHOD

1 Heat the oil in a frying pan; fry the aubergine till golden brown.

2 Take 1 tbsp oil in a separate pot; add salt, bay leaf, cumin seeds, cinnamon stick, cloves, and 4 cups water. Add fennel powder, ginger powder, and cumin powder; bring to the boil. Add yoghurt and keep stirring until it is mixed well with the gravy.

3 Add fried aubergine and cook for 5 minutes. Sprinkle black cumin seeds and green cardamom powder; mix well.

4 Serve hot garnished with green chillies, accompanied with steamed rice or chapatti or *nan*.

Note: While serving make sure the aubergines don't break.

Razma Hemb t, Wangen

FRENCH BEANS WITH AUBERGINE

Serves: 6

INGREDIENTS

1 kg / 2.2 lb French beans, washed, stringed, cut into 2″ pieces
250 gm / 9 oz Aubergine (*baigan*), small ones, washed, cut into 4 pieces
½ cup / 110 ml / 3½ fl oz Refined / Mustard oil for frying
2 tbsp / 30 ml / 1 fl oz Oil for cooking
1 tsp / 2 gm Cumin (*jeera*) seeds
Salt to taste
2 tsp / 6 gm Red chilli powder
1 tsp / 3 gm Ginger powder (*sonth*)
1 tsp / 3 gm *Ver* masala (see p. 16)
4 Dried red chillies (*sookhi lal mirch*)

METHOD

1 Heat the oil in a frying pan; fry the aubergine and keep aside.

2 Take 2 tbsp oil in a separate pan; add French beans, cumin seeds, and salt; stir well and cook for 10 minutes over high heat. Add red chilli powder and ginger powder; stir and simmer for 10 minutes.

3 Add *ver* masala, dried red chillies, and fried aubergine; stir once and serve hot with *nan*.

Tchont t, Wangen

COOKING APPLES WITH AUBERGINE

Serves: 6

INGREDIENTS

500 gm / 1.1 lb Cooking apples, washed, cut into 4 pieces, deseeded, do not peel
250 gm / 9 oz Aubergine (*baigan*), long ones, washed, cut into 4 pieces
½ cup / 110 ml / 3½ fl oz Mustard / Refined oil for frying
1 tbsp / 15 ml Oil for cooking
Salt to taste
1 tsp / 3 gm Red chilli powder
½ tsp / 1½ gm Ginger powder (*sonth*)
½ tsp / 1½ gm Turmeric (*haldi*) powder
3 Green chillies

METHOD

1 Heat the oil in a pan; fry the aubergine until crispy brown. Remove and keep aside.

2 Fry the apples in the same oil, turning once. Remove them carefully so that they do not break.

3 Take 1 tbsp oil in a separate pan; add salt, red chilli powder, ginger powder, turmeric powder, and 2 cups water. Bring to the boil. Add fried apples and aubergine and cook for 2 minutes over high heat. Add green chillies and serve hot with steamed rice.

Souchal t, Wangen

KASHMIRI SPINACH WITH AUBERGINE

Serves: 6

INGREDIENTS

1 kg / 2.2 lb Kashmiri Spinach (*haak*),
  discard the hard stems, washed, drained
250 gm / 9 oz Aubergine (*baigan*), small, cut
  into 4 pieces, washed, drained
½ cup / 110 ml / 3½ fl oz Mustard oil
½ tsp Asafoetida (*hing*)
Salt to taste
2 tsp / 6 gm Red chilli powder
4 Dried red chillies (*sookhi lal mirch*)
1 tsp / 3 gm *Ver* masala (see p. 16)

METHOD

1 Heat the oil in a pan; fry the aubergine
   until brown. Keep aside.

2 In the same oil, add asafoetida, salt, and
   Kashmiri spinach; stirring until the leaves
   are a little tender.

3 Add red chilli powder and mix well. Add
   fried aubergine and dried red chillies; mix.
   Sprinkle *ver* masala mix and serve hot.

Tamater t, Wangen

TOMATOES WITH AUBERGINE

Serves: 6

INGREDIENTS

1 kg / 2.2 lb Aubergine (*baigan*), long ones,
  washed, cut length wise into 2 pieces
700 gm / 25 oz Tomatoes, chopped
2 cups / 440 ml / 15 fl oz Refined oil for
  frying
3 tsp / 9 gm Red chilli powder
½ tsp / 1½ gm Cumin (*jeera*) seeds
2 tsp / 6 gm Ginger powder (*sonth*)
Salt to taste
5 Green chillies

METHOD

1 Heat the oil in a deep-frying pan; fry the
   aubergine until light brown. Keep aside.

2 Take 1 tbsp oil in a separate pot; add
   tomatoes and cook for 10 minutes. Add red
   chilli powder, cumin seeds, 4 cups water,
   ginger powder, and salt; bring to the boil.

3 Add the fried aubergine and green chillies;
   cook over high heat for 5 minutes.

4 Serve hot with steamed rice or any thing of
   your choice.

'If there is heaven on Earth, it is here, it is here, it is
here,' uttered Jehangir when he first set his eyes upon
Kashmir in the seventeenth century. The beautiful
Chinar (maple) trees and their leaves lend a touch
of gold to the Mughal Gardens in Srinagar.
Photograph: Mukhtar Ahmad

Tchok Wangen

TANGY AUBERGINE

Serves: 6

INGREDIENTS

1 kg / 2.2 lb Aubergine (*baigan*), long ones,
   cut into 4 long pieces, washed, drained
2 cups / 440 ml / 15 fl oz Mustard oil for
   frying
2 Cloves (*laung*)
Salt to taste
3 tsp / 9 gm Red chilli powder
1 tsp / 3 gm Ginger powder (*sonth*)
2 tsp / 6 gm Fennel (*saunf*) powder
1 tsp / 3 gm *Ver* masala (see p. 16)
½ cup / 100 ml / 3½ fl oz Tamarind liquid
5 Green chillies

METHOD

1 Heat the oil in a deep-frying pan; fry the
   aubergine until golden brown. Set aside.

2 In a separate vessel, take 2 tbsp oil; add
   cloves, salt, red chilli powder, and 4 cups
   water. Add the rest of the spices and
   tamarind liquid; bring to the boil.

3 Add the fried aubergine and cook over
   high heat for 5 minutes.

4 Serve hot garnished with green chillies and
   accompanied with steamed rice.

Al Rogan Josh

PUMPKIN IN RED GRAVY

Serves: 6

INGREDIENTS

1 kg / 2.2 lb Pumpkin (*kaddu*), peeled, cut
   into pieces 3 cm wide
2 cups / 440 ml / 15 fl oz Mustard /
   Refined oil for frying
½ tsp Asafoetida (*hing*)
2 Cloves (*laung*)
2 Black cardamom (*badi elaichi*), crushed
1 Cinnamon (*dalchini*) stick
Salt to taste
3 tsp / 9 gm Red chilli powder
2 tsp / 6 gm Ginger powder (*sonth*)
3 tsp / 9 gm Fennel (*saunf*) powder
1½ cups / 335 gm / 11½ oz Yoghurt (*dahi*),
   whisked well
1 tsp / 2½ gm Black cumin (*shah jeera*) seeds
3 Green cardamoms (*choti elaichi*), crushed

METHOD

1 Heat the oil in a deep pan; deep-fry the
   pumpkin until golden brown.

2 Take 3 tbsp oil in another vessel; add cloves,
   asafoetida, black cardamom, cinnamon
   stick, salt, red chilli powder, 2 cups water,
   ginger powder, and fennel powder. Bring
   to the boil. Add yoghurt and keep stirring.
   Add the fried pumpkin and cook until the
   gravy thickens.

3 Sprinkle black cumin seeds and green
   cardamom powder and simmer for 2
   minutes. Remove and serve hot.

Al Yakhni

BOTTLE GOURD IN YOGHURT

Serves: 6

INGREDIENTS

1 kg / 2.2 lb Bottle gourd (*lauki*), peeled,
  cut into 3 cm-long and 2 cm-wide pieces
2 cups / 450 gm / 1 lb Yoghurt (*dahi*),
  whisked
2 cups / 440 ml / 15 fl oz Mustard /
  Refined oil for frying
2 tbsp / 30 ml Oil for cooking
2 Cinnamon (*dalchini*) sticks
3 Cloves (*laung*)
2 Bay leaves (*tej patta*)
1 tsp / 2 gm Cumin (*jeera*) seeds
Salt to taste
3 tsp / 9 gm Fennel (*saunf*) powder
2 tsp / 6 gm Ginger powder (*sonth*)
2 Black cardamoms (*badi elaichi*), crushed
2 tsp / 5 gm Black cumin (*shah jeera*) seeds
3 Green cardamoms (*choti elaichi*), crushed

METHOD

1 Heat the oil in pan; deep-fry the bottle
   gourd in hot oil until golden brown.

2 Take 2 tbsp oil from the pan in a separate
   vessel; add cinnamon sticks, cloves, bay
   leaves, cumin seeds, salt, 3 cups water,
   fennel powder, and ginger powder. Bring
   to the boil. Add yoghurt and stir well with
   a ladle. Add the fried bottle gourd and
   cook until the gravy thickens. Sprinkle
   black cumin seeds and green cardamom
   powder; mix well.

3 Serve with rice or chapatti.

*A villager smoking
a hookah outside
his house.
Photograph:
Mukhtar Ahmad*

Kanguch Yakhni

MORELS IN YOGHURT SAUCE

Serves: 6

INGREDIENTS

250 gm / 9 oz Mushrooms (*morels*), washed,
  cleaned, soaked in warm water for 30 minutes
½ cup / 110 ml / 3½ oz Mustard oil
2 Cloves (*laung*)
½ tsp Asafoetida (*hing*)
1 Cinnamon (*dalchini*) stick
1 Bay leaf (*tej patta*)
Salt to taste
2 tsp / 6 gm Fennel (*saunf*) powder
1 tsp / 3 gm Ginger powder (*sonth*)
1 tsp / 3 gm Cumin (*jeera*) powder
500 gm / 1.1 lb Yoghurt (*dahi*), whisked
2 Black cardamoms (*badi elaichi*), crushed
4 Green cardamoms (*choti elaichi*), crushed
1 tsp / 2½ gm Black cumin (*shah jeera*) seeds

METHOD

1 Heat the oil in a pot; add cloves, asafoetida
  cinnamon stick, bay leaf, salt, and
  mushrooms. Fry for a few minutes. Pour
  2 cups water and fennel powder, ginger
  powder, and cumin powder. Cook until
  the mushrooms are tender.

2 Add whisked yoghurt and keep stirring
  gently so that the mushrooms do not break.

3 Add black and green cardamoms and black
  cumin seeds. Simmer for 5 minutes or until
  the gravy thickens.

4 Serve with steamed rice, chapatti or *nan*.

*Note: This is a special kind of wild mushroom
found in the hills of Kashmir.*

Phool Rogan Josh

CAULIFLOWER IN THICK RED GRAVY

Serves: 6

INGREDIENTS

1 kg / 2.2 lb Cauliflower (*phool gobi*), cut
  into single florets
2 cups / 440 ml / 15 fl oz Mustard /
  Refined oil for frying
3 tbsp / 45 ml / 1½ fl oz Oil for cooking
½ tsp Asafoetida (*hing*)
2 Cloves (*laung*)
1 Cinnamon (*dalchini*) stick
1 Bay leaf (*tej patta*)
Salt to taste
3 tsp / 6 gm Red chilli powder
½ cup / 110 gm / 3½ oz Yoghurt (*dahi*),
  whisked
2 tsp / 6 gm Fennel (*saunf*) powder
1 tsp / 3 gm Ginger powder (*sonth*)
1 tsp / 2 gm Cumin (*jeera*) seeds
1 tsp / 3 gm Black cardamom (*badi elaichi*)
  powder

METHOD

1 Heat the oil in a pan; fry the cauliflower
  until crispy brown.

2 Heat 3 tbsp oil in a pot; add asafoetida,
  cloves, cinnamon stick, bay leaf, salt, red
  chilli powder, and yoghurt. Stir well. Add
  2 cups water, fennel powder, ginger powder,
  and cumin seeds; boil over high heat. Add
  fried cauliflower and cook until the gravy
  turns thick. Sprinkle black cardamom
  powder.

3 Serve with steamed
  rice, chapatti
  or *nan*.

Kanguch t, Chaman

MORELS AND COTTAGE CHEESE IN YOGHURT

Serves: 6

INGREDIENTS

250 gm / 9 oz Mushrooms (*morels*), soaked in warm water for 30 minutes
500 gm / 1.1 lb Cottage cheese (*paneer*), cut into medium-sized pieces
1 cup / 220 ml / 7 fl oz Mustard / Refined oil
2 Cloves (*laung*)
½ tsp Asafoetida (*hing*)
1 tsp / 2 gm Cumin (*jeera*) seeds
1 tsp / 3 gm Turmeric (*haldi*) powder
3 tsp / 9 gm Fennel (*saunf*) powder
2 tsp / 6 gm Ginger powder (*sonth*)
1 tsp / 3 gm Cumin powder
Salt to taste
2 tsp / 6 gm Fenugreek (*methi*) powder
½ cup / 110 gm / 3½ oz Yoghurt (*dahi*), whisked

METHOD

1 Fry the cottage cheese in hot oil until light brown. Keep aside.

2 Take 3 tbsp oil from the same pan; add cloves, asafoetida, cumin seeds and mushrooms. Cook for 5 minutes. Add 4 cups water and all the powdered spices; bring to the boil. Add fried cottage cheese and cook over medium heat until the gravy thickens.

3 Add whisked yoghurt just before serving.

4 Serve with steamed rice, *nan* or chapatti.

Chaman t Meeth

COTTAGE CHEESE IN FENUGREEK SAUCE

Serves: 6

INGREDIENTS

500 gm / 1.1 lb Cottage cheese (*paneer*), sliced into 1″-thick square pieces
250 gm / 9 oz Fenugreek (*methi*), cleaned, washed
½ cup / 110 ml / 3½ fl oz Mustard / Refined oil
1/3 tsp Asafoetida (*hing*)
Salt to taste
2 tsp / 6 gm Red chilli powder
1 tsp / 3 gm Ginger powder (*sonth*)
1 tsp / 3 gm Turmeric (*haldi*) powder
2 Cloves (*laung*)

METHOD

1 Boil fenugreek in a large vessel for 10 minutes. Drain the water and keep aside to cool. Mash with hands or grind in a mixer.

2 Heat the oil in a pan; fry the cottage cheese and keep aside.

3 In the same oil, add asafoetida, salt and fenugreek and fry for 2 minutes. Add red chilli powder and all other spices.

4 Add 3 cups water and bring to the boil. Add fried cottage cheese (optional, you can just add cottage cheese without frying) and cook for 10 minutes until the gravy thickens.

5 Serve with the main course.

Wangen Hetch, Tamber Lagith

DRIED AUBERGINE IN TAMARIND SAUCE

Serves: 6

INGREDIENTS

250 gm / 9 oz Dried Aubergine (*baigan*), washed
½ cup / 100 ml / 3½ fl oz Tamarind (*imli*) liquid
½ cup / 110 ml / 3½ fl oz Mustard oil
Salt to taste
½ tsp Asafoetida (*hing*)
2 tsp / 6 gm Red chilli powder
1 tsp / 2 gm Cumin (*jeera*) seeds
1 tsp / 3 gm Ginger powder (*sonth*)
1 tsp / 3 gm Fennel (*saunf*) powder
1 tsp / 3 gm *Ver* masala (see p. 16)

METHOD

1 Boil the aubergine in a pot with 8 cups water until half tender. Remove and squeeze gently. Keep aside and make sure they do not break.

2 Heat the oil in a separate vessel; add salt, asafoetida, and aubergine; fry until light brown. Add red chilli powder, cumin seeds, 4 cups water, ginger powder, and fennel powder; cook for 2 minutes over high heat. Add tamarind liquid and boil for a minute. Add *ver* masala; mix well.

3 Serve hot with steamed rice.

Al Hetch in Zamudud

DRIED BOTTLE GOURD IN YOGHURT

Serves: 6

INGREDIENTS

250 gm / 9 oz Dried bottle gourd (*lauki*), washed
4 tbsp / 60 ml / 2 fl oz Mustard oil
Salt to taste
½ tsp Asafoetida (*hing*)
1 Bay leaf (*tej patta*)
2 Cloves (*laung*)
1 tsp / 3 gm Ginger powder (*sonth*)
2 tsp / 6 gm Fennel (*saunf*) powder
1 tsp / 2 gm Cumin (*jeera*) seeds
2 cups / 450 gm / 1 lb Yoghurt (*dahi*), whisked
1 tsp / 2½ gm Black cumin (*shah jeera*) seeds
2 Green cardamoms (*choti elaichi*), crushed

METHOD

1 Boil the bottle gourd in a pot with 8 cups water until half tender. Remove and squeeze gently. Keep aside.

2 Heat the oil in a pot; add salt, asafoetida, bay leaf, cloves, and bottle gourd. Cook for 2 minutes. Add 2 cups water, ginger powder, fennel powder, and cumin seeds. Boil over high heat till the gravy thickens.

3 Add whisked yoghurt and stir well. Add black cumin seeds and crushed green cardamom.

4 Serve hot with steamed rice.

Haak t, Chaman

KASHMIRI SPINACH WITH COTTAGE CHEESE

Serves: 6

INGREDIENTS

1 kg / 2.2 lb Kashmiri Spinach (*haak*),
  cleaned, washed
500 gm / 1.1 lb Cottage cheese (*paneer*),
  sliced into 2″-long x ½″-thick, square pieces
1 cup / 220 ml / 7 fl oz Mustard oil
½ tsp Asafoetida (*hing*)
Salt to taste
2 Cloves (*laung*)
2 tsp / 6 gm Turmeric (*haldi*) powder
2 tsp / 6 gm Ginger powder (*sonth*)
3 tsp / 9 gm Fennel (*saunf*) powder
5 Green chillies

METHOD

1 Heat the oil in a deep pan; fry the cottage
   cheese until light brown. Keep aside.

2 Take same leftover oil in a pressure cooker;
   add asafoetida, salt, cloves, 8 cups water,
   turmeric powder, ginger powder, and fennel
   powder. Bring to the boil over high heat.

3 Add Kashmiri spinach and pressure cook
   for 5 minutes. Remove the lid, add fried
   cottage cheese and cook until the cheese
   becomes soft.

4 Serve hot, garnished with green chillies.

Thool Razma Yakhni

GREEN KIDNEY BEANS IN YOGHURT

Serves: 6

INGREDIENTS

1 kg / 2.2 lb Green beans, shelled
¼ cup / 55 ml / 1¾ fl oz Refined /
  Mustard oil
Salt to taste
½ tsp Asafoetida (*hing*)
2 Cloves (*laung*)
1 Bay leaf (*tej patta*)
3 tsp / 9 gm Fennel (*saunf*) powder
2 tsp / 6 gm Ginger powder (*sonth*)
2 cups / 450 gm / 1 lb Yoghurt (*dahi*), whisked
2 Black cardamoms (*badi elaichi*), crushed
3 Green cardamoms (*choti elaichi*), crushed
½ tsp / 1¼ gm Black cumin (*shah jeera*) seeds
½ tsp Asafoetida

METHOD

1 Heat the oil in a pressure cooker; add
   asafoetida, the green beans, salt, cloves,
   and bay leaf. Fry for 5 minutes. Add 3 cups
   water, fennel powder, and ginger powder.
   Pressure cook for 2 minutes.

2 Add whisked yoghurt and mix well. Add
   crushed black and green cardamoms and
   black cumin seeds; mix well. Serve hot.

Karel t, Wangen Dued Lagith

BITTER GOURD AND AUBERGINE IN YOGHURT

Serves: 6

INGREDIENTS

500 gm / 1.1 lb Bitter gourd (*karela*),
  scraped, cut lengthwise, deseeded
250 gm / 9 oz Aubergine (*baigan*), small,
  washed, cut into 2 pieces
1 cup / 225 gm / 8 oz Yoghurt (*dahi*),
  whisked
½ cup / 110 ml / 3½ fl oz Mustard /
  Refined oil
2 Cloves (*laung*)
¼ tsp Asafoetida (*hing*)
1 tsp / 3 gm Ginger powder (*sonth*)
2 tsp / 6 gm Fennel (*saunf*) powder
Salt to taste
1 tsp / 3 gm Cumin (*jeera*) powder
1 tsp / 2 gm Cumin seeds
3 Green chillies

METHOD

1 Sprinkle salt all over the bitter gourd and
   keep aside for an hour. Wash and squeeze
   water from the bitter gourd with your
   palm.

2 Heat the oil in a frying pan; fry the
   aubergine until light brown. Remove and
   fry the bitter gourd in the same oil.

3 Take the leftover oil in a separate pot; add
   cloves, asafoetida, 2 cups water, all the
   powered spices, and cumin seeds. Bring to
   the boil. Add yoghurt, stirring and mixing
   well with the gravy.

4 Add fried bottle gourd and aubergine; cook
   for 5 minutes or until the gravy thickens.

5 Serve hot, garnished with green chillies
   and accompanied with steamed rice or
   chapatti.

Gurdol t, Oluv

RAW PLUM WITH POTATOES

Serves: 6

INGREDIENTS

500 gm / 1.1 lb Raw plums (*gurdol*), washed
1 kg / 2.2 lb Potatoes, peeled, washed, cut
    into 6 pieces
3 tbsp / 45 ml / 1½ fl oz Mustard /
    Refined oil
2 tsp / 6 gm Red chilli powder
Salt to taste
2 tsp / 6 gm Ginger powder (*sonth*)
6 Green chillies

METHOD

1 Heat the oil in a deep pan; add the potatoes
   and fry for 10 minutes. Add red chilli
   powder, salt, 4 cups water, and ginger
   powder; cook until the potatoes are tender.

2 Add the plums to the potato mixture and
   bring to the boil. Cook until the plums are
   tender.

3 Remove and garnish with green chillies.
   Serve with steamed rice.

Verifol t, Oluv

SUN-DRIED BLACK LENTILS WITH POTATOES

Serves: 6

INGREDIENTS

100 gm / 3½ oz Dried black gram
    dumplings (*vadi*), washed, drained quickly
    to avoid getting soggy
500 gm / 1.1 lb Potatoes, peeled, washed,
    cut into 6 pieces
3 tbsp / 45 ml / 1½ fl oz Mustard /
    Refined oil
2 tsp / 6 gm Red chilli powder
1 tsp / 3 gm Ginger powder (*sonth*)
Salt to taste
½ cup / 110 gm / 3½ oz Yoghurt (*dahi*),
    whisked

METHOD

1 Heat the oil in a deep pot; fry the dumplings
   for 2 minutes. Remove to a plate.

2 Fry the potatoes in the same oil for
   5-10 minutes. Add red chilli powder,
   4 cups water, ginger powder, and salt. Add
   fried dumplings and cook until tender.

3 Add whisked yoghurt and cook until the
   gravy thickens.

4 Serve with steamed rice or chapatti.

Al Kanej t, Wangen

PUMPKIN GREENS WITH AUBERGINE

Serves: 6

INGREDIENTS

1 kg / 2.2 lb Pumpkin greens, discard long
  rough stems, washed, drained
250 gm / 9 oz Aubergine (*baigan*), long
  ones, cut into 6 pieces, washed, drained
½ cup / 110 ml / 3½ fl oz Mustard oil
½ tsp Asafoetida (*hing*)
Salt to taste
3 tsp / 9 gm Red chilli powder
2 tsp / 6 gm Ginger powder (*sonth*)
2 tsp / 6 gm *Ver* masala (see p. 16)
5 Dried red chillies (*sookhi lal mirch*)

METHOD

1 Heat the oil in a pan; fry the aubergine
   until light brown. Remove.

2 In the same oil, add asafoetida, salt, and
   pumpkin greens; mix well with a ladle
   and fry until the water dries up and it is
   half tender.

3 Add red chilli powder, ginger powder,
   and *ver* masala; keep stirring. Add fried
   aubergine and dried red chillies. Cook for
   a minute.

4 Serve with steamed rice.

Note: This dish is a speciality of Kashmir cuisine.

Muj Pattar t, Wangen

RADISH LEAVES WITH AUBERGINE

Serves: 6

INGREDIENTS

1 kg / 2.2 lb Radish (*mooli*) with leaves,
  scraped, diced
250 gm / 9 oz Aubergine (*baigan*), long
  ones, washed, cut into 4 pieces
½ cup / 110 ml / 3½ fl oz Mustard oil
  for frying
2 tbsp / 30 ml / 1 fl oz Oil for cooking
½ tsp Asafoetida (*hing*)
5 Dried red chillies (*sookhi lal mirch*)
Salt to taste
1 tsp / 3 gm *Ver* masala (see p. 16)

METHOD

1 Clean the radish leaves separately by cutting
   the stems out. Wash well.

2 Put 8 cups water in a pressure cooker. Add
   radish and leaves together and pressure
   cook for 15 minutes or until 4 whistles.
   Remove the lid and wash the steamed
   radish and leaves under running tap water
   and squeeze gently. Keep aside.

3 Heat the oil in a frying pan; fry the
   aubergine until light brown.

4 Heat 2 tbsp oil in a vessel; add asafoetida,
   salt, and squeezed leaves and radish; fry for
   5 minutes. Pour 6 cups water and bring to
   the boil. Add dried red chillies, salt, and
   fried aubergine; cook for 5 minutes and
   sprinkle *ver* masala.

5 Serve hot.

*Facing page: Sunset in the Dal Lake – truly
overpowering and awe inspiring!
Photograph: Wajid Drabu*

96

*A typical village scene in autumn when
chillies are left in the sun to dry.*

RICE & BREAD

100   BATHA
Steamed rice

100   MATTAR TAHER
Yellow rice

101   NENI PULAO
Lamb pulao

102   TAHER T, CHARVAN
Yellow rice with liver

102   MODUR PULAO
Sweet rice with dry fruits

103   KANGACH PULAO
Mushroom pulao

103   SHAKER PARE
Bread made of chestnut flour

105   CHER CHOT
Rice flour pancakes

105   ROTH
Sweet fried flour breads

Batha

STEAMED RICE

Serves: 6

INGREDIENTS

1 kg / 2.2 lb Basmati rice, washed
10 cups / 2.5 lt Water

METHOD

1 Mix rice and water in a large vessel and bring to the boil. When the rice is half cooked, drain all the water and continue to cook over low heat for 15 minutes.

2 Serve hot.

Note: By discarding the water the calorie content reduces. I will not suggest to absorb the water as done usually.

Mattar Taher

YELLOW RICE

Serves: 6

INGREDIENTS

3 cups / 600 gm / 22 oz Rice, washed
200 gm / 7 oz Green peas (*hara mattar*), peeled
½ tsp / 1½ gm Turmeric (*haldi*) powder
Salt to taste
2 tbsp / 30 ml / 1 fl oz Mustard oil, heated

METHOD

1 Boil the peas in a pot for 5 minutes and drain out the water.

2 Cook the rice in a vessel with 8 cups water. Add turmeric powder and mix well with a ladle. Bring to the boil, add peas and boil together until half tender; drain out the water.

3 Return to heat and cook on low heat for 15 minutes.

4 In a large plate transfer the yellow rice and mix with oil and salt.

5 Serve with pickles.

Note: Taher *is cooked on birthdays and special occasions in Pandit homes.*

Neni Pulao

LAMB PULAO

Serves: 6-8

INGREDIENTS

1 kg / 2.2 lb Basmati rice, washed, soaked, drained
700 gm / 25 oz Lamb
2 tsp / 6 gm Turmeric (*haldi*) powder
2 tsp / 6 gm Ginger powder (*sonth*)
Salt to taste
4 Cloves (*laung*)
2 Bay leaves (*tej patta*)
2 tsp / 4 gm Cumin (*jeera*) seeds
6 Green cardamoms (*choti elaichi*), crushed
6 Green chillies, cut into pieces
½ tsp Saffron (*kesar*)
3 Onions, chopped, fried brown
⅓ cup Ghee / Refined oil
4 Black cardamoms (*badi elaichi*), crushed

METHOD

1 Put the lamb in a pressure cooker with 6 cups water, turmeric powder, ginger powder, salt, cloves, bay leaves, and cumin seeds. Pressure cook for 10 minutes. Remove from heat and keep aside to cool.

2 Boil rice separately in 12 cups water. When half tender, drain the water out completely.

3 Open the lid of the cooker and in a separate large vessel mix the drained rice and lamb together. Add crushed green cardamom and green chillies in layers. Top with saffron, onions, and ghee/refined oil. Sprinkle crushed black cardamom and cook over low heat for 30 minutes.

4 Serve with *kabargah* (see p. 43) and any kind of pickle.

The cool and calm grandeur of winter snow in Srinagar.

Taher t, Charvan
YELLOW RICE WITH LIVER

Serves: 6

INGREDIENTS

1 kg / 2.2 lb Rice
500 gm / 1.1 lb Liver, cut into cubes, washed, drained
3 tbsp / 45 ml / 1½ fl oz Mustard oil
Salt to taste
2 tsp / 6 gm Red chilli powder
2 tsp / 6 gm Turmeric (*haldi*) powder

METHOD

1 Heat 2 tbsp oil in a deep pot; add liver and fry until dark brown. Add salt, red chilli powder, 1 tsp turmeric powder and 2 cups water; cook until the liver is tender. Remove from heat.

2 Boil rice with 1 tsp turmeric powder separately. When rice is half cooked, drain out the water. Return to heat and cook on low heat for 15 minutes.

3 In a large pot, mix the rice and liver together and serve with *munj aanchar* (see p.114).

Modur Pulao
SWEET RICE WITH DRY FRUITS

Serves: 6

INGREDIENTS

1 kg / 2.2 lb Rice, washed
1 cup / 200 gm / 7 oz Sugar
4 Green cardamoms (*choti elaichi*), crushed
4 Black cardamoms (*badi elaichi*), crushed
2 tsp Saffron (*kesar*)
2 cups / 400 gm / 14 oz Ghee
½ cup / 70 gm / 2¼ oz Raisins (*kishmish*), soaked, washed
½ cup / 70 gm / 2¼ oz Almonds (*badam*), soaked, peeled
¼ cup / 20 gm Dry coconut (*nariyal*), pared, shredded
⅓ cup Dry dates *(khajur)*, deseeded, cut length wise
4 Cloves (*laung*)
2 Bay leaves (*tej patta*)
2 Cinnamon (*dalchini*) sticks

METHOD

1 Boil the rice in 10 cups water. When half cooked, drain all the water out. Remove from heat.

2 Boil the sugar in 3 cups water to make syrup. Add green and black cardamoms. Add saffron and boil until the sugar dissolves completely.

3 Heat the ghee in a pan; add raisins, almonds, coconut, dates, cloves, bay leaves, and cinnamon sticks and sauté. Add half cooked rice and the syrup; mix well and cook over very low heat for 30 minutes.

4 Serve hot.

Kangach Pulao

MOREL PULAO

Serves: 6

INGREDIENTS

3 cups / 600 gm / 22 oz Basmati rice,
  soaked for 10 minutes
100 gm / 3½ fl oz Morels (guchhi), soaked
  for 10 minutes,
6 tbsp / 90 ml / 3 fl oz Refined oil / Ghee
4 Cloves (laung)
5 Green cardamoms (choti elaichi)
5 Black cardamoms (badi elaichi)
2 Bay leaves (tej patta)
½ cup / 70 gm / 2¼ oz Almonds (badam),
  blanched
Salt to taste
2 tsp / 6 gm Ginger powder (sonth)
½ tsp / 1½ gm Turmeric (haldi) powder
1 tsp Saffron (kesar) extract

METHOD

1 Heat the ghee / oil in a heavy-bottomed
   pot; add, cloves, green and black
   cardamoms, bay leaves, and almonds; stir
   for 2 minutes. Add salt and mushrooms; fry
   for 2–3 minutes.

2 Add soaked rice and stir well. Add 3 cups
   water, ginger powder, turmeric powder,
   salt, and saffron extract; mix well and
   simmer. Cook, covered, until the rice and
   mushrooms are cooked well.

3 Serve hot.

Shaker Pare

SWEET BREAD MADE OF CHESTNUT FLOUR

Serves: 6

INGREDIENTS

1 kg / 2.2 lb Chestnut (sin gaada) flour
2 cups / 400 gm / 14 oz Sugar
1¼ cups / 250 gm / 9 oz Ghee
3 cups / 660 ml / 21 fl oz Refined oil
  for frying

METHOD

1 Boil the sugar in a deep pot with 2 cups
   water until the sugar dissolves completely.
   Remove from heat and keep aside to cool.

2 Mix the ghee with the flour and knead
   with warm sugar syrup.

3 Roll the dough out to make a thick chapatti.
   Cut with a knife into square pieces (this is
   called shaker pare).

4 Heat the oil in a pan; deep-fry the shaker
   pare until brown. Remove and keep aside
   to cool. Then store in an airtight jar and
   enjoy whenever you wish.

Note: This snack is made in Pandit festivals
especially on thread ceremony. This snack is
meant for those who are fasting. You can make
salty shaker pare also by using salt instead
of sugar.

The floating vegetable gardens on the Dal Lake.

Cher Chot

RICE FLOUR PANCAKES

Serves: 4

INGREDIENTS

1 cup / 100 gm / 3½ oz Rice flour
Salt to taste
½ tsp / 1¼ gm Black cumin (*shah jeera*) seeds
½ cup / 110 ml / 3½ fl oz Refined oil

METHOD

1 Mix the rice flour with 1 cup water and make a thick paste of dropping consistency.

2 Add salt and black cumin seeds and mix well.

3 Heat about 1 tsp oil in a non-stick frying pan; put ½ cup rice flour mixture in the pan and spread evenly. Fry both sides, turning upside down, until golden brown and crisp. Remove and repeat till all the batter is used up.

4 Serve with *kehwa* (see p. 120) or any other kind of tea.

Roth

SWEET FRIED FLOUR BREAD

Serves: 6

INGREDIENTS

1 kg / 2.2 lb Refined flour (*maida*)
1½ cups / 300 gm / 11 oz Sugar
1 cup / 200 gm / 7 oz Ghee for mixing
5 Black cardamoms (*badi elaichi*), coarsely ground
Refined oil / Ghee for deep-frying
½ cup Poppy seeds (*khus khus*)

METHOD

1 Heat 4 cups water, add sugar and boil until the sugar dissolves completely. Remove and keep aside to cool.

2 In a large bowl, add flour, ghee, black cardamom, and the sugar syrup. Knead well and make a hard dough.

3 Take some dough about 3-4″-thick and roll out into a circular chapatti. Make flowery designs with a toothpick or a fork / spoon.

4 Heat the oil / ghee in a pan; deep-fry the chapatti over low heat until golden brown. Remove and quickly sprinkle poppy seeds on one side. Repeat until all are fried.

5 Serve with *sheer chai* (see p. 120).

Note: Roth is prepared in the Pandit festival of Pun which falls in the month of September. It is a must for everyone in the family to get a share. I always look forward to this festival to enjoy roth.

Scarlet chillies festoon the windows of village homes.
A unique way of drying chillies in Kashmir!
Photograph: Mukhtar Ahmad

CHUTNEYS & PICKLES

Anardan Chetin

POMEGRANATE CHUTNEY

Serves: 6

INGREDIENTS

1 cup Pomegranate (*anar dana*)
Salt to taste

METHOD

1 Wash pomegranate thoroughly.

2 Grind in a grinder or in a mortar
   and pestle.

3 Add salt to taste and serve.

Muj Chetin Doud Dhar

GRATED RADISH IN YOGHURT

Serves: 6

INGREDIENTS

500 gm / 1.1 lb Radish (*mooli*), washed,
   scraped, grated, squeezed
½ cup / 110 gm / 3½ oz Yoghurt (*dahi*),
   whisked
3 Green chillies, deseeded, cut into
   small pieces
Salt to taste
½ tsp Black cumin (*shah jeera*) seeds

METHOD

In a bowl, mix yoghurt, radish, green chillies,
and salt together. Sprinkle black cumin seeds
and serve.

Note: This can be served as a side dish any time.
If you want it spicy, add ½ tsp red chilli powder.

Gurdol Chetin

PLUM CHUTNEY

Serves: 6

INGREDIENTS

500 gm / 1.1 lb Plum *(gurdol)*, deseeded
½ tsp / 1½ gm Red chilli powder
Salt to taste

METHOD

1 Put plum, red chilli powder, and salt in a mixer. Grind for a second.

2 Enjoy this chutney with any thing of your choice.

Aalch Chetin

SOUR CHERRY CHUTNEY

Serves: 6

INGREDIENTS

1 cup Cherries, deseeded, washed
Salt to taste
½ tsp / 1½ gm Red chilli powder

METHOD

1 Crush the cherries with your hands and remove the seeds.

2 Add salt and red chilli powder. Mix well.

3 Serve with steamed rice, chapatti, *nan* or even pulao.

Doon Chetin

WALNUT CHUTNEY

Serves: 6

INGREDIENT

1 cup / 120 gm / 4 oz Walnuts (*akhrot*),
   shelled, soaked in warm water for 2 hours,
   skin peeled
4 Green chillies
2 cups / 450 gm / 1 lb Yoghurt (*dahi*)
Salt to taste
½ tsp / 1¼ gm Black cumin (*shah jeera*) seeds

METHOD

1 Grind walnuts and green chillies to a
   fine paste.

2 Mix yoghurt and salt in a bowl. Add the
   walnut paste and mix well.

3 Refrigerate for 30 minutes before serving.

Note: This can be used as a dip for cocktail salads.

Buzith Nadir Chetin

ROASTED LOTUS STEM CHUTNEY

Serves: 6

INGREDIENTS

500 gm / 1.1 lb Lotus stems (*kamal kakri*),
   cut into 5 cm pieces, washed
1 Onion, medium-sized, chopped
2 Green chillies, deseeded
Salt to taste
⅓ cup Tamarind (*imli*) liquid
2 Lemon (*nimbu*) juice

METHOD

1 Roast the lotus stems on the gas or in a
   microwave. Grill for 10 minutes on each
   side.

2 Grind the lotus stems with onion, green
   chillies, and salt. Add lemon juice or
   tamarind liquid; mix well and serve.

Facing page: Autumn time, Dal Lake.
Photograph: S. Irfan

Talith Muj Chetin
FRIED RADISH CHUTNEY

Serves: 6

INGREDIENTS

1 kg / 2.2 lb Radish (*mooli*), washed, scraped, grated
3 tbsp / 45 ml / 1½ fl oz Mustard / Refined oil
Salt to taste
⅓ tsp Asafoetida (*hing*)
2 tsp / 6 gm Red chilli powder
1 tsp / 3 gm Ginger powder (*sonth*)
1 tsp / 2½ gm Black cumin (*shah jeera*) seeds
5 Dried red chillies (*sookhi lal mirch*), deseeded
½ tsp / 1½ gm *Ver* masala (see p. 16)

METHOD

1 Squeeze the water out from the grated radish.

2 Heat the oil in a pan; add salt, asafoetida, and grated radish. Keep stirring until the remaining water dries up. Add red chilli powder and ginger powder; fry for a minute. Sprinkle black cumin seeds, dried red chillies, and *ver* masala; mix well.

3 Enjoy the chutney with chapatti, rice or *nan*.

Note: Serve this chutney with haak *or any green vegetables.*

Sabz Badam Aanchar
GREEN ALMOND PICKLE

Serves: 6

INGREDIENTS

1 kg / 2.2 lb Green baby almonds (*badam*), washed, pat-dried
1 cup / 220 ml / 7 fl oz Mustard oil
3 tsp / 9 gm Black mustard (*rai*) seeds
Salt to taste
3 tsp / 9 gm Red chilli powder

METHOD

1 Mix oil, black mustard seeds, salt, and red chilli powder together in a pot.

2 Add green almonds and mix.

3 Put in an airtight jar and keep in the sun for a week.

4 Serve with all kinds of meals, vegetarian or non-vegetarian.

Note: This pickle is a delicacy of Kashmir cuisine.

Wazul Saboot Marchwangen Aanchar

WHOLE RED CHILLI PICKLE

Serves: 6-10

INGREDIENTS

1 kg / 2.2 lb Red chillies (*lal mirch*), fresh,
   washed, pat-dried
1 cup / 220 ml / 7 fl oz Mustard oil
3 tsp / 9 gm Red chilli powder
½ cup Black mustard seeds (*rai*)
Salt to taste

METHOD

1 Prick the chillies with a knife.

2 Mix all the spices and chillies together and
   put in a jar.

3 Tighten the jar and keep in the sun for a
   week and serve.

Snowfall in Srinagar.
Photograph: S. Irfan

Munj Aanchar

KNOL KHOL PICKLE

Serves: 6

INGREDIENTS

1 kg / 2.2 lb Knol khol (*kholrabi*), washed
2 cups / 440 ml / 15 fl oz Mustard oil [raw]
5 tsp / 15 gm Red chilli powder
3 tsp / 9 gm Ginger powder (*sonth*)
1 cup Black mustard (*rai*) seeds
Salt to taste

METHOD

1 Separate the leaves from the balls of the knol khol and cut into 2-3 pieces each. Peel and cut the balls into 5-6 cm piece. Keep the knol khol and leaves to dry in the kitchen for 1 day in summer months and 2 days in winters so that the moisture evaporates totally. There should be no water left.

2 Put 2 cups of unheated mustard oil in a deep vessel. Add red chilli powder, ginger powder, black mustard seeds, and salt. Add dried knol khol. Mix thoroughly until the spices are well mixed.

3 Transfer contents into an airtight jar. Keep in the sun for about a week.

4 Serve with non-vegetarian and vegetarian dishes.

Cher Aanchar

APRICOT PICKLE

Serves: 6

INGREDIENTS

1 kg / 2.2 lb Apricot (*khubani*), slightly hard to touch, washed, pat-dried
1½ cups / 330 ml / 11 fl oz Mustard Oil [raw]
3 tsp / 9 gm Red chilli powder
1 cup Black mustard (*rai*) seeds
Salt to taste

METHOD

1 Prick the apricots with a fork.

2 Mix oil, red chilli powder, black mustard seeds, and salt in a pot. Add apricot to the mixture and transfer into an airtight jar.

3 Keep the jar in the sun for 4-5 days.

4 Serve with any kind of dishes.

Note: This pickle is very typical of Kashmir. Make sure the apricot is not soft.

A view of the city enveloped by thick snow blanket. Photograph: S. Irfan

A tea break in the field.
Photograph: Mukhtar Ahmad

DESSERTS

Kheer

RICE PUDDING

Serves: 6

INGREDIENTS

½ cup / 100 gm / 3½ oz Basmati rice,
 soaked overnight
8 cups / 2 lt / 64 fl oz Full-cream milk, boiled
2 cups / 400 gm / 14 oz Sugar
¼ cup / 35 gm / 1¼ oz Almonds (*badam*),
 soaked, peeled
⅓ cup Raisins (*kishmish*)
¼ cup / 20 gm Dry coconut (*nariyal*), shredded
6 Cashew nuts (*kaju*), crushed
1 tsp Saffron (*kesar*)
5 Green cardamoms (*choti elaichi*), crushed

METHOD

1 Crush the soaked rice with your hands and
 put in a deep vessel. Pour 4 cups water and
 boil until the rice is mixed well with the
 water.

2 Add milk and boil, stirring continuously,
 till it is mixed well and the consistency is
 thick. Add sugar, keep mixing with a ladle.

3 Add all the dry fruits, saffron, and crushed
 green cardamom; mix well. Bring to the
 boil and simmer for 20 minutes. Remove
 and keep aside to cool.

4 Serve chilled.

Phirin

SEMOLINA GARNISHED WITH DRY FRUITS

Serves: 6

INGREDIENT

½ cup / 100 gm / 3½ oz Semolina (*suji*),
 soaked for 1 hour
4 cups / 1 lt / 32 fl oz Full-cream milk,
 boiled
½ cup / 100 gm / 3½ oz Sugar
2 tbsp Cashew nuts (*kaju*), crushed
6 Almonds (*badam*), soaked, peeled
2 tbsp Pistachios (*pista*), crushed
½ tsp Saffron (*kesar*)

METHOD

1 Boil semolina in 2 cups water until it is
 mixed well with water. Add milk and
 bring to the boil, stirring constantly.

2 Add dry fruits and saffron and boil until the
 mixture thickens. Simmer for 20 minutes
 stirring well. Remove and serve chilled.

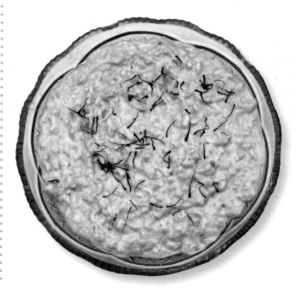

Shufta

SWEETENED COTTAGE CHEESE WITH DRY FRUITS

Serves: 6

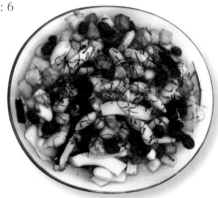

INGREDIENTS

250 gm / 9 oz Cottage cheese (*paneer*), cut
   into ½ cm cubes
½ cup / 110 ml / 3½ fl oz Refined oil / Ghee
1 cup / 200 gm / 7 oz Sugar
½ cup / 40 gm / 1¼ oz Coconut (*nariyal*),
   fresh, chopped
½ cup / 70 gm / 2¾ oz Almonds (*badam*),
   peeled
½ cup / 70 gm / 2¾ oz Raisins (*kishmish*)
6 Green cardamoms (*choti elaichi*), crushed
½ tsp Saffron, soaked in 2 tsp warm water

METHOD

1 Heat the oil in a deep pan; deep-fry the
   cottage cheese and keep aside.

2 Boil the sugar in 6 cups water. Add the fried
   cottage cheese and boil for 5 more minutes.

3 Heat 1 tbsp oil in a frying pan; fry the
   coconut and almonds for 1-2 minutes. Add
   to the boiling cottage cheese. Add raisins,
   green cardamoms and saffron extract and
   boil for another 3 minutes. Remove and
   cool to room temperature. Serve with the
   main course or as a dessert.

*Note: This dish is cooked only on special occasions
like weddings, festivals, etc. This is Lata
Mangeshkar's favourite dish among many others.*

Top: Carrying earthenware in wicker baskets.
Below: Embroidering a shawl with Kashmiri motifs.

119

Sheer Chai

PINK SALTY TEA

Serves: 6

INGREDIENTS

1 tsp *Kehwa* tea leaves
¼ tsp Sodium bicarbonate
2 cups / 480 ml / 16 fl oz Milk
Salt to taste
2 tsp Cream of boiled milk
2 Almonds (*badam*), crushed
2 Green cardamoms (*choti elaichi*), crushed

METHOD

1 Boil 1 cup water, soda bicarbonate, and tea leaves in a pot for 10 minutes.

2 If the water starts drying up, add 1 more cup of water. Keep boiling till the colour of the tea turns dark.

3 Add 1 more cup of water, milk, and salt. Bring to the boil.

4 Strain into cups. Add little bit of cream on top, crushed almonds and green cardamom. Serve after meals.

Note: This tea acts as a digestive after a heavy meal.

Kehwa

KASHMIRI GREEN TEA

Serves: 6

INGREDIENTS

1 tsp *Kehwa* tea leaves, crushed
Sugar to taste
4 Green cardamoms (*choti elaichi*), crushed
1 tsp / 3 gm Cinnamon (*dalchini*) powder
6 Almonds (*badam*), crushed

METHOD

1 Boil 6 cups water in a pot. Add sugar to taste followed by tea leaves.

2 Add crushed green cardamom and cinnamon powder; mix well.

3 Strain the mixture into individual tea cups.

4 Sprinkle crushed almonds on the cups and serve.

Note: Traditionally this tea is served after dinner and at breakfast. It is very good for curing cough and cold and can be enjoyed anytime.

Facing page: The backwaters of Srinagar about a 100 years ago.

*Hari Parbat Fort in Srinagar on top with the famous Hazrat
Makhdoom Sahib Shrine on the left. This shrine attracts thousands
of pilgrims everyday as it is reputed for its healing power.
Photograph: Mukhtar Ahmad*

LOW CALORIE RECIPES

Varimooth t, Gogje
BLACK KIDNEY BEANS WITH TURNIPS

Serves: 6-8

INGREDIENTS

1 kg / 2.2 lb Black kidney beans, soaked
  overnight, drained
4-6 pieces Turnips (*shalgam*), peeled,
  washed, cut into 4-6 pieces
1 tbsp / 15 ml Mustard oil
½ tsp Asafoetida (*hing*)
Salt to taste
3 tsp / 9 gm Red chilli powder
2 tsp / 6 gm Ginger powder (*sonth*)
2 tsp / 6 gm *Ver* masala (see p. 16)
5 Dried red chillies (*sookhi lal mirch*)

METHOD

1 Heat the oil in a pressure cooker; add
asafoetida, salt, 20 cups water, kidney beans,
red chilli powder, and ginger powder.
Pressure cook for 5 minutes.

2 Open the lid and add turnips and pressure
cook again for 5 minutes. Let it cool down,
add *ver* masala, stir well and boil until the
turnips and beans are tender. (The gravy in
this dish should be thin.)

Olav Dude Legit
POTATOES IN YOGHURT

Serves: 6

INGREDIENTS

1 kg / 1.1 lb Potatoes, peeled, washed, cut
  into 1″-thick, round pieces
1 cup / 225 gm / 8 oz Yoghurt (*dahi*),
  whisked
1 tbsp / 15 ml Refined oil
2 Cloves (*laung*)
1 Bay leaf (*tej patta*)
2 tsp / 6 gm Turmeric (*haldi*) powder
2 tsp / 6 gm Ginger powder (*sonth*)
2 tsp / 4 gm Cumin (*jeera*) seeds
Salt to taste
1 tsp / 2½ gm Black cumin (*shah jeera*) seeds

METHOD

1 Heat the oil in a deep vessel; add potatoes,
cloves, and bay leaf. Fry for 5 minutes. Add
4 cups water, turmeric powder, ginger
powder, cumin seeds, and salt; cook until
the potatoes are tender.

2 Add yoghurt and mix well. Add black
cumin seeds and simmer for 2 minutes.

3 Serve the way you like.

T Chat Gogje

TURNIPS IN LIGHT GRAVY

Serves: 6

INGREDIENTS

1 kg / 2.2 lb Turnips (*shalgam*), peeled,
  washed, sliced
1 tbsp / 15 ml Refined oil
¼ tsp Asafoetida (*hing*)
Salt to taste
5 Dried red chillies (*sookhi lal mirch*)
½ tsp / 1½ gm *Ver* masala (see p. 16)

METHOD

1 Heat the oil in a pressure cooker; add asafoetida, salt, and turnips; stir. Add ½ cup water and pressure cook for 10 minutes.

2 Open the lid and pour 4 cups water. Add dried red chillies and *ver* masala; cook over high heat until the gravy thickens.

3 Serve hot.

Gogje t, Nadir

TURNIPS WITH LOTUS STEMS

Serves: 6

INGREDIENTS

1 kg / 2.2 lb Turnips (*shalgam*), peeled,
  washed, shredded
500 gm / 1.1 lb Lotus stems (*kamal kakri*),
  scraped, washed, cut into horizontal pieces
1 tbsp / 15 ml Mustard / Refined oil
¼ tsp Asafoetida (*hing*)
Salt to taste
4 Dried red chillies (*sookhi lal mirch*),
  deseeded
1 tsp / 3 gm *Ver* masala (see p. 16)

METHOD

1 Heat the oil in a pressure cooker; add asafoetida, salt, turnips, and lotus stems. Pour ½ cup water, mix well and pressure cook for 5 minutes.

2 Open the lid and cook over high heat, stirring occasionally. Add 4 cups water and dried red chillies, cook until both the turnips and lotus stems are tender.

3 Add *ver* masala and mix well.

4 Serve hot.

Potters working on a heavy wheel!

Phool t, Nadir
CAULIFLOWER WITH LOTUS STEMS

Serves: 6

INGREDIENTS

1 kg / 2.2 lb Cauliflower (*phool gobi*), cut
  into florets, washed, drained
250 gm / 9 oz Lotus stems (*kamal kakri*),
  scraped, washed, cut into 2″-long pieces
1 tbsp / 15 ml Refined oil
½ tsp Asafoetida (*hing*)
Salt to taste
3 tsp / 9 gm Red chilli powder
2 tsp / 6 gm Ginger powder (*sonth*)
1 tsp / 2 gm Cumin (*jeera*) seeds

METHOD

1 Heat the oil in a pressure cooker; add
  asafoetida, salt, cauliflower, and lotus stems.
  Cook over high heat for 5 minutes. Add
  red chilli powder, ginger powder, cumin
  seeds, and ½ cup water; pressure cook for
  5 minutes or till one whistle.

2 Open the lid quickly and your dish is
  ready to serve.

Moung Dal Dhulee
SIMPLE GREEN GRAM

Serves: 6

INGREDIENTS

2½ cups / 500 gm / 1.1 lb Green gram
  (*moong dal*), washed
½ tsp Refined oil
¼ tsp Asafoetida (*hing*)
Salt to taste
1 tsp / 3 gm Turmeric (*haldi*) powder
1 tsp / 3 gm Ginger powder (*sonth*)
1 tsp / 2 gm Cumin (*jeera*) seeds
4 Green chillies

METHOD

1 Heat the oil in a deep pot; add asafoetida,
  salt, 6 cups water, turmeric powder, ginger
  powder, and cumin seeds. Cook on high
  heat till the lentil is well mixed and soft.

2 Add green chillies and simmer for 5 minutes.
  Remove.

3 Serve with steamed rice, chapatti or *nan*.

Chana Dal
FLAVOURED BENGAL GRAM

Serves: 6

INGREDIENTS

2½ cups / 500 gm / 1.1 lb Bengal gram
  (*chana dal*), washed, soaked for 1 hour
1 tsp / 5 ml Refined oil
½ tsp Asafoetida (*hing*)
Salt to taste
1 tsp / 3 gm Turmeric (*haldi*) powder
2 tsp / 6 gm Ginger powder (*sonth*)
1 tsp / 2 gm Cumin (*jeera*) seeds
1 tsp / 3 gm Fennel (*saunf*) powder
4 Green chillies

METHOD

1 Heat the oil in a pressure cooker; add
   asafoetida, salt, 6 cups water, turmeric
   powder, ginger powder, cumin seeds,
   fennel powder, and Bengal gram. Pressure
   cook for 15 minutes.

2 Open the lid and check if the Bengal gram
   is tender and mixed well.

3 Remove and garnish with green chillies.
   Serve hot.

Moung Dal Chilka t, Gogje
GREEN SPLIT LENTILS WITH TURNIPS

Serves: 6

INGREDIENTS

2½ cups / 500 gm / 1.1 lb Green gram
  (*moong dal*), split
250 gm / 9 oz Turnips (*shalgam*), peeled,
  washed, cut into 6″ pieces
1 tbsp / 15 ml Mustard oil
½ tsp Asafoetida (*hing*)
Salt to taste
1 tsp / 3 gm Turmeric (*haldi*) powder
1 tsp / 3 gm Ginger powder (*sonth*)
2 tsp / 6 gm Fennel (*saunf*) powder
5 Dried red chillies (*sookhi lal mirch*)

METHOD

1 Heat the oil in a pressure cooker; add
   asafoetida, salt, 8 cups water, turmeric
   powder, ginger powder, fennel powder,
   green gram, and turnips. Pressure cook for
   10 minutes.

2 Open the lid and add dried red chillies.
   Cook for 5 minutes and serve hot.

A couple walks amidst heavy snowfall in Srinagar.
Photograph: S. Irfan

Moung Dal t, Muj

WHOLE GREEN LENTIL WITH RADISH

Serves: 6

INGREDIENTS

1 kg / 2.2 lb Whole Green gram (*moong dal*), soaked for 15 minutes
500 gm / 1.1 lb Radish (*mooli*), peeled, cut into 3″ pieces
Salt to taste
½ tsp Asafoetida (*hing*)
2 tsp / 6 gm Turmeric (*haldi*) powder
2 tsp / 6 gm Ginger powder (*sonth*)
3 tsp / 9 gm Fennel (*saunf*) powder
1 tsp / 2 gm Cumin (*jeera*) seeds
4 Dried red chillies (*sookhi lal mirch*)
1 tbsp / 15 ml Mustard oil

METHOD

1 Heat the oil in a pressure cooker; add radish and fry for 2 minutes.

2 Add soaked green gram along with 8 cups water, salt, asafoetida, turmeric powder, ginger powder, fennel powder, and cumin seeds; stir and pressure cook for 10 minutes.

3 Remove from heat, open the lid when it cools down. Return to heat and bring the mixture to the boil. Add dried red chillies and serve hot.

Moung Dal t, Nadir

WHOLE GREEN LENTIL WITH LOTUS STEMS

Serves: 6-8

INGREDIENTS

1 kg / 2.2 lb Whole Green gram (*moong dal*), soaked for 15 minutes
500 gm / 1.1 lb Lotus stems (*kamal kakri*), scraped, cut into 3″-long pieces, cleaned under tap water
2 tsp / 6 gm Turmeric (*haldi*) powder
2 tsp / 6 gm Ginger powder (*sonth*)
3 tsp / 9 gm Fennel (*saunf*) powder
Salt to taste
½ tsp Asafoetida (*hing*)
2 tsp / 4 gm Cumin (*jeera*) seeds
5 Dried red chillies (*sookhi lal mirch*), deseeded
1 tsp / 5 ml Mustard oil, optional

METHOD

1 Add soaked green gram in a pressure cooker with 8 cups water, lotus stems, oil, turmeric powder, ginger powder, fennel powder, salt, asafoetida, and cumin seeds; mix well with a ladle and pressure cook for 10 minutes.

2 After it cools down open the lid of cooker and bring the mixture to the boil until it is mixed well.

3 Add dried red chillies and boil for 2 minutes. Serve hot.

Ruins of a temple at Martand.

Muj Mulvin

RADISH GREENS

Serves: 6

INGREDIENTS

1 kg / 2.2 lb Radish (*mooli*) with leaves,
  leaves cut and cleaned, radish scraped
  and sliced
1 tbsp / 15 ml Mustard oil
¼ tsp Asafoetida (*hing*)
Salt to taste
4 Dried red chillies (*sookhi lal mirch*)
½ tsp *Ver* masala (see p. 16)

METHOD

1 Put 4 cups water in a pressure cooker. Add
   radish and leaves together; pressure cook
   for 15 minutes.

2 Open the lid and drain the water out. Wash
   under a tap and squeeze properly.

3 Heat the oil in a deep pot; add asafoetida,
   salt, and the radish with leaves. Stir well
   and pour 6 cups water. Bring to the boil
   and add dried red chillies and *ver* masala;
   mix well.

4 Serve hot with steamed rice

Razma Hembh t, Nadir

STIR FRIED FRENCH BEANS WITH LOTUS STEMS

Serves: 6

INGREDIENTS

1 kg / 2.2 lb French beans, stringed, cut into
  2, washed
200 gm / 7 oz Lotus stems (*kamal kakri*),
  scraped, cut into ½″-thick rounds, washed
  thoroughly
2 tbsp / 30 ml / 1 fl oz Mustard / Refined /
  Olive oil
Salt to taste
¼ tsp Asafoetida (*hing*)
1 tsp / 2 gm Cumin (*jeera*) seeds
2 tsp / 6 gm Red chilli powder
1 tsp / 3 gm Ginger powder (*sonth*)
3 Dried red chillies (*sookhi lal mirch*), deseeded

METHOD

1 Heat the oil in a pan; add salt, asafoetida,
   cumin seeds, French beans, and lotus stems.
   Stir and cook over high heat for 5 minutes.
   Add red chilli powder and ginger powder;
   mix well and simmer for 15 minutes,
   stirring occasionally until the beans and
   lotus stems are tender.

2 Add the dried red chillies and mix.

3 Serve with chapatti or any thing of your
   choice.

Hedder Yakhni

MUSHROOMS IN YOGHURT

Serves: 6

INGREDIENTS

1 kg / 2.2 lb Mushroom, cut into half, washed
2 cups / 450 gm / 1 lb Yoghurt (*dahi*), whisked
1 tsp / 5 ml Mustard / Refined / Olive oil
2 Bay leaves (*tej patta*)
2 Cloves (*laung*)
1 Cinnamon (*dalchini*) stick
Salt to taste
3 tsp / 9 gm Fennel (*saunf*) powder
2 tsp / 6 gm Ginger powder (*sonth*)
1 tsp / 2½ gm Black cumin (*shah jeera*) seeds

METHOD

1 Boil the mushrooms in 3 cups water for 5 minutes; drain well.

2 Heat the oil in a deep pot; add bay leaves, cloves, cinnamon stick, and salt. Add mushrooms and fry for 5 minutes.

3 Add 4 cups water, fennel powder, and ginger powder. Cook for 2 minutes. Add yoghurt and mix well; cook until the gravy thickens.

4 Sprinkle black cumin seeds and serve hot.

Note: Do not add water in this vegetable. It is cooked in its own moisture, tastes delicious and is high in fibre.

Razma Hembh t, Gand

FRENCH BEANS WITH ONIONS

Serves: 6

INGREDIENTS

1 kg / 2.2 lb French beans, stringed, cut into 2, washed
200 gm / 7 oz Onions, peeled, cut into pieces
2 tbsp / 30 ml / 1 fl oz Mustard / Refined / Olive oil
Salt to taste
¼ tsp Asafoetida (*hing*)
2 tsp / 6 gm Red chilli powder
1 tsp / 3 gm Ginger powder (*sonth*)
1 tsp / 2 gm Cumin (*jeera*) seeds
5 Dried red chillies (*sookhi lal mirch*), deseeded

METHOD

1 Heat the oil in a pan; add salt, asafoetida, beans, and onions. Stir on high heat for 5 minutes. Simmer and add red chilli powder, ginger powder, and cumin seeds. Mix well.

2 Add dried red chillies and simmer until the beans are tender.

3 Serve with chapatti, *nan,* or any thing of your choice.

Note: Cook this vegetable over low heat and without any water as it cooks in its own miosture.

Chaman Kaliya

COTTAGE CHEESE IN YELLOW GRAVY

Serves: 6-8

INGREDIENTS

1 kg / 2.2 lb Cottage cheese (*paneer*),
cut into 1"-thick, square pieces
1 tbsp / 15 ml Mustard / Refined /
Olive oil
1 Bay leaf (*tej patta*)
1 Cinnamon (*dalchini*) stick
2 Cloves (*laung*)
Salt to taste
2 tsp / 6 gm Turmeric (*haldi*) powder
2 tsp / 6 gm Ginger powder (*sonth*)
3 tsp / 9 gm Fennel (*saunf*) powder
1 tsp / 3 gm Cumin (*jeera*) powder
1 cup / 240 ml / 8 fl oz Milk, skimmed,
boiled
4 Green cardamom (*choti elaichi*), crushed

METHOD

1 Heat the oil in a deep pot; add bay leaf, cinnamon stick, cloves, salt, and 8 cups water. Bring to the boil and add turmeric powder, ginger powder, fennel powder, and cumin powder; mix well.

2 Add cottage cheese and cook until the cheese is soft and the gravy thickens.

3 Add milk and cook for 2 minutes. Sprinkle crushed green cardamom and mix well.

4 Serve hot.

Note: This dish is low in calories because the cottage cheese is not fried which is normally done. And the oil used is only 1 tsp. Cottage cheese is a good source of calcium.

Left: Dal Lake
Right: A break on a long journey about a 100 years ago

131

Razma t, Gogje

KIDNEY BEANS WITH TURNIPS

Serves: 6

INGREDIENTS

1 kg / 2.2 lb Kidney beans (*rajma*), soaked
   overnight, drained
250 gm / 9 oz Turnips (*shalgam*), peeled,
   washed, cut into 4 pieces
½ tsp Asafoetida (*hing*)
Salt to taste
3 tsp / 9 gm Red chilli powder
2 tsp / 6 gm Ginger powder (*sonth*)
2 tsp / 6 gm *Ver* masala (see p. 16)

METHOD

1 Pressure cook soaked beans in 15 cups fresh
   water for 5 minutes.

2 Open the lid, add turnip, asafoetida, salt,
   red chilli powder, and ginger powder; mix
   well. Again pressure cook for 5 minutes.

3 Add *ver* masala and bring to the boil.

4 Serve with rice or anything of your choice.

Kokur t, Tureel

CHICKEN WITH SNAKE GOURD

Serves: 6

INGREDIENTS

1 kg / 2.2 lb Chicken, boneless or with
   bones, washed
2 kg / 4.4 lb Snake gourd (*turai*), scraped,
   cut into medium-sized pieces, washed
2 tbsp / 30 ml / 1 fl oz Mustard oil /
   Refined / Olive oil
Salt to taste
½ tsp Asafoetida (*hing*)
1 tsp / 2 gm Cumin (*jeera*) seeds
2 tsp / 6 gm Turmeric (*haldi*) powder
3 tsp / 9 gm Fennel (*saunf*) powder
2 tsp / 6 gm Ginger powder (*sonth*)
1 tsp / 3 gm Cumin powder

METHOD

1 Heat the oil in a deep pot; add salt,
   asafoetida, cumin seeds, and chicken. Stir
   for 10 minutes over high heat. Add snake
   gourd and mix well. Add all the powdered
   spices and 4 cups water; stir and cook until
   the gravy is thick and chicken is tender.

2 Serve garnished with green chillies and
   accompanied with steamed rice or chapatti.

Kokur Yakhni

CHICKEN IN YOGHURT

Serves: 6

INGREDIENTS

1 kg / 2.2 lb Chicken, leg and thigh pieces
3 cups / 675 gm / 24 oz Yoghurt (*dahi*),
  whisked made of skimmed milk
2 tbsp / 30 ml / 1 fl oz Mustard / Refined /
  Olive oil
½ tsp Asafoetida (*hing*)
Salt to taste
2 Bay leaves (*tej patta*)
2 Cloves (*laung*)
2 Cinnamon (*dalchini*) sticks
2 tsp / 6 gm Ginger powder (*sonth*)
3 tsp / 9 gm Fennel (*saunf*) powder
1 tsp / 3 gm Cumin (*jeera*) powder
5 Green cardamoms (*choti elaichi*), crushed
2 Black cardamoms (*badi elaichi*), crushed
1 tsp / 2½ gm Black cumin (*shah jeera*) seeds

METHOD

1 Heat the oil in a deep vessel; add asafoetida,
   salt, bay leaves, cloves, cinnamon sticks,
   and chicken; stir for 10 minutes. Add 6
   cups water, ginger powder, fennel powder,
   and cumin powder; cook until the chicken
   is tender. Remove from heat.

2 Transfer the gravy from the cooked chicken
   into a separate pot. Add yoghurt and bring
   to the boil; stirring well. Add crushed
   green and black cardamoms and sprinkle
   black cumin seeds; mix well.

3 Pour this gravy back into the chicken and
   bring to the boil. Remove.

4 Serve hot.

Kokur Kaliya

CHICKEN KALIYA

Serves: 6

INGREDIENTS

1 kg / 2.2 lb Chicken, cut into 12 pieces,
  washed
1 tbsp / 15 ml Mustard / Refined / Olive oil
½ tsp Asafoetida (*hing*)
Salt to taste
2 Cloves (*laung*)
2 Bay leaves (*tej patta*)
2 Cinnamon (*dalchini*) sticks
2 tsp / 6 gm Ginger powder (*sonth*)
1½ tsp / 4½ gm Turmeric (*haldi*) powder
3 tsp / 9 gm Fennel (*saunf*) powder
2 tsp / 4 gm Cumin (*jeera*) seeds
1 cup / 240 ml / 8 fl oz Skimmed milk (boiled)
4 Green cardamoms (*choti elaichi*), crushed
2 Black cardamoms (*badi elaichi*), crushed

METHOD

1 Heat the oil in a deep pot; add asafoetida,
   salt, cloves, bay leaves, cinnamon sticks,
   and chicken. Stir for 5 minutes. Add 6 cups
   water, ginger powder, turmeric powder,
   fennel powder, and cumin seeds; cook over
   high heat until the chicken is tender.

2 Add milk and bring to the boil. Add
   crushed green and black cardamoms; mix.

3 Serve hot.

The Dal Lake famous for its houseboats and shikaras is surrounded by the snow-capped mountains.
Photograph: Mukhtar Ahmad

Buzith Kokur
GRILLED CHICKEN

Serves: 6

INGREDIENTS

1 kg / 2.2 lb Chicken, leg and thigh pieces,
  washed, drained
1 cup / 225 gm / 8 oz Yoghurt (*dahi*)
Salt to taste
2 tsp / 12 gm Ginger (*adrak*) paste
2 tsp / 12 gm Garlic (*lasan*) paste
2 tsp / 6 gm Cumin (*jeera*) powder
2 tsp / 6 gm Red chilli powder
1 tbsp / 15 ml Olive oil

METHOD

1 In a bowl, mix yoghurt, salt, ginger and
   garlic pastes, cumin powder, red chilli
   powder, olive oil, and chicken together.
   Marinate for 2 hours.

2 Preheat oven to 180°C / 350°F and grill the
   chicken till golden brown, or grill in the
   microwave.

3 Serve with chapatti or *nan*.

A chilly winter evening by the Dal Lake.
Photograph: S. Irfan

Kokur Kabab
CHICKEN KEBAB

Serves: 6

INGREDIENTS

1 kg / 2.2 lb Chicken mince, done 4 times
  in mixer
Salt to taste
2 tsp / 12 gm Ginger (*adrak*) paste
1 tsp / 6 gm Garlic (*lasan*) paste
3 tsp / 9 gm Red chilli powder
1 tsp / 2½ gm Black cumin (*shah jeera*) seeds
2 tsp / 6 gm Black cardamoms (*badi elaichi*)
  powder
4 Green chillies, chopped
1 tbsp / 15 ml Refined oil
⅓ cup Green coriander (*hara dhaniya*) leaves,
  chopped
2 tbsp Dry mint leaves

METHOD

1 Put the mince in a bowl. Add salt, ginger
   paste, garlic paste, red chilli powder, cumin
   seeds, black cardamom powder, green
   chillies, and oil; mix well with your hands.

2 Divide the mixture into equal portions and
   mould one portion on a skewer pressing
   with your palm and finger shaping into
   a sausage. Grill on charcoal fire or in
   microwave oven for 10 minutes, turning
   around carefully. Repeat till all are grilled.

Kokur Shyami

CHICKEN CUTLETS IN YOGHURT

Serves: 6-8

INGREDIENTS

1 kg / 2.2 lb Chicken mince
2 tsp / 6 gm Ginger powder (*sonth*)
3 tsp / 9 gm Fennel (*saunf*) powder
2 tsp / 4 gm Cumin (*jeera*) seeds
Salt to taste
2 tsp / 6 gm Black cardamoms (*badi elaichi*)
  powder [for mixing]
2 tbsp / 30 ml / 1 fl oz Refined oil
3 Cloves (*laung*)
2 Cinnamon (*dalchini*) sticks
2 Bay leaves (*tej patta*)
3 cups / 675 gm / 24 oz Yoghurt (*dahi*),
  made of skimmed milk, whisked
2 tsp / 5 gm Black cumin (*shah jeera*) seeds
3 Black cardamoms, crushed
4 Green cardamoms (*choti elaichi*), crushed

METHOD

1 Put the mince in a bowl. Add 1 tsp ginger
   powder, 1 tsp fennel powder, 1 tsp cumin
   seeds, ½ tsp salt, and black cardamom
   powder; mix well.

2 Divide the mixture into equal portions
   and shape into 2″-long and 1″-thick, round
   cutlets.

3 Heat the oil in a large pot; add cloves,
   cinnamon sticks, bay leaves, and 6 cups
   water. Bring to the boil. Add the remaining
   spices and boil. Add cutlets and cook over
   high heat until the gravy thickens.

4 Add yoghurt and cook, stirring occasionally,
   until the gravy thickens.

5 Garnish with black cumin seeds and crushed
   black and green cardamoms. Serve hot.

Buzith Kabargah

GRILLED LAMB CHUNKS

Serves: 6

INGREDIENTS

1 kg / 2.2 lb Lamb, cut from breast in
  squares, washed
2 cups / 480 ml / 15 fl oz Skimmed milk,
  boiled
1 Bay leaf (*tej patta*)
1 Cinnamon (*dalchini*) stick
2 Cloves (*laung*)
4 Green cardamoms (*choti elaichi*), crushed
2 Black cardamoms (*badi elaichi*), crushed
¼ tsp Fennel (*saunf*) powder
1 tsp / 3 gm Ginger powder (*sonth*)
1 tsp / 3 gm Cumin (*jeera*) powder
Salt to taste
¼ tsp Saffron (*kesar*) extract

METHOD

1 In a pressure cooker, add the meat,
   2 cups water, milk, bay leaf, cinnamon
   stick, cloves, crushed green and brown
   cardamom, fennel powder, ginger powder,
   cumin powder, salt, and saffron. Pressure
   cook for 10 minutes.

2 Remove from heat and check if the meat is
   tender. Cook over high heat again until the
   gravy is absorbed completely.

3 Take out the meat pieces with a tong
   carefully so that they do not break.

4 Preheat oven to 180°C / 350°F and grill the
   meat till golden brown or in a microwave,
   grill for 20 minutes on each side turning
   carefully.

5 Serve hot and decorate on a bed of lettuce.

Bandh T, Syun
CABBAGE WITH MEAT

Serves: 6

INGREDIENTS

1 kg / 2.2 lb Lamb, cut from shoulder
1 kg / 2.2 lb Cabbage (*bandh gobi*), cut into
full pieces, washed well
2 tbsp / 30 ml / 1 fl oz Mustard /
Refined oil
½ tsp Asafoetida (*hing*)
Salt to taste
1 tsp / 2 gm Cumin (*jeera*) seeds
2 tsp / 6 gm Turmeric (*haldi*) powder
2 tsp / 6 gm Ginger powder (*sonth*)
3 tsp / 9 gm Fennel (*saunf*) powder
1 tsp / 3 gm Cumin powder
5 Green chillies

METHOD

1 Heat the oil in a pressure cooker; add
asafoetida, salt, cumin seeds, and lamb.
Cook over high heat for 10 minutes.
Pressure cook for 5 minutes.

2 Open the lid, add cabbage, mix well with a
ladle and cook over high heat. Add 4 cups
water and all the powdered spices; stir well.
Pressure cook for 5 minutes.

3 Serve garnished with green chillies.

*The Shalimar Garden was built for Nur Jahan by
her husband Jehangir in 1616. The top most of
the four terraces, called the 'Abode of Love', was
reserved for the emperor and the ladies of court.*

Buzith Syun
GRILLED LAMB

Serves: 6

INGREDIENTS

1 kg / 2.2 lb Lamb, cut from leg
1 cup / 225 gm / 8 oz Yoghurt (*dahi*)
2 tsp / 12 gm Garlic (*lasan*) paste
2 tsp / 12 gm Ginger (*adrak*) paste
1 tbsp / 15 ml Olive / Refined oil
Salt to taste
2 tsp / 6 gm Red chilli powder
1 tsp / 3 gm Cumin (*jeera*) powder
3 tbsp / 45 gm / 1½ oz Papaya paste
1 tbsp / 15 ml Cooking vinegar

METHOD

1 In a deep bowl, mix yoghurt with garlic and
ginger pastes, oil, salt, red chilli powder,
cumin powder, papaya paste, and vinegar;
mix well.

2 Add lamb, mix well and marinate for
12 hours.

3 Preheat the oven to 180°C / 350°F and grill
the lamb until golden brown. Or grill in
the microwave oven until golden brown.

Buzith Mach

GRILLED LAMB CUTLETS

Serves: 6

INGREDIENTS

1 kg / 2.2 lb Minced lamb
1 tbsp / 15 gm Yoghurt (*dahi*)
2 tsp / 6 gm Red chilli powder
1 tsp / 3 gm Ginger powder (*sonth*)
2 tsp / 6 gm Cumin (*jeera*) powder
Salt to taste
1 tbsp / 15 ml Mustard oil

METHOD

1 In a deep bowl, mix yoghurt, minced meat, red chilli powder, ginger powder, cumin powder, salt, and oil together; mix well and marinate for 1 hour.

2 Divide the mixture into equal portions and shape into round or rectangular cutlets.

3 Grill the cutlets in a microwave until brown or grill in a preheated oven at 180°C / 350°F till brown.

4 Serve as a snack or with the main course.

Buzith Gaad

GRILLED FISH

Serves: 6

INGREDIENTS

1 kg / 2.2 lb Fish (Sole), boneless, cut into
    square or rectangular pieces
2 tbsp / 30 ml / 1 fl oz Lemon (*nimbu*) juice
1 tsp / 3 gm Red chilli powder
1 tsp / 6 gm Ginger (*adrak*) paste
1 tsp / 6 gm Garlic (*lasan*) paste
1 tsp / 3 gm Cumin (*jeera*) powder
1 tbsp / 15 ml Olive oil
Salt to taste

METHOD

1 Mix all the ingredients together and marinate the fish for 1 hour.

2 Grill the fish in a microwave until golden brown. Turning once.

3 Serve hot.

Note: Chicken can also be cooked in the same way.

Chinar trees draped in snow in Srinagar.
Photograph: S. Irfan

Gaad Kaliya
FISH IN YELLOW GRAVY

Serves: 6

INGREDIENTS

1 kg / 2.2 lb Fish (*Sole / Rohu / Singada*),
   cut into slices
2 tsp / 6 gm Turmeric (*haldi*) powder
2 tbsp / 30 ml / 1 fl oz Mustard oil
Salt to taste
1 tsp / 2 gm Cumin (*jeera*) seeds
½ tsp Asafoetida (*hing*)
3 tsp / 9 gm Fennel (*saunf*) powder
2 tsp / 6 gm Ginger powder (*sonth*)
5 Green chillies

METHOD

1 Sprinkle 1 tsp turmeric powder all over the
   fish and keep aside for 1 hour.

2 Heat the oil in a pressure cooker; add salt,
   cumin seeds, asafoetida, 6 cups water, 1
   tsp turmeric powder, fennel powder, and
   ginger powder. Bring to the boil, add fish
   and pressure cook for 5 minutes.

3 Open the lid and add green chillies. Cook
   again over high heat for 5 minutes. Serve
   with rice.

A potter at work in the 1920s.

*One of the several bridges
on the River Jhelum.*

All photographs courtesy Sarla Razdan

ISBN: 978-81-941109-4-1

© Sarla Razdan, 2020

Published in India by
Roli Books Pvt Ltd
M-75, Greater Kailash-II Market
New Delhi 110 048, India
Phone: ++91-11-4068 2000
Email: info@rolibooks.com
Website: www.rolibooks.com

Editor: Neeta Datta
Cover design: Sneha Pamneja
Design: Supriya Saran, Divya Bhardwaj
Production: Lavinia Rao

Printed and bound in
Nutech Print Services, India